THE FIRST EASTER
by PETER MARSHALL
Edited and with introduction by Catherine Marshall

JESUS LOVED THEM
by SAM PATRICK and OMAR GARRISON
Living portraits of people who knew Jesus

GUIDEPOSTS ASSOCIATES, INC., Carmel, N.Y.

About these two books ...

In these confusing times it is somehow deeply satisfying and refreshing when old truths come vividly to life for us. To find this kind of spiritual nourishment people in ever increasing numbers are turning to the Bible, to Bible commentaries and to books of inspiration based on Scripture.

Here Guideposts brings two of these books together in a single exciting volume. Peter Marshall's *The First Easter* and *Jesus Loved Them* by artist Sam Patrick and newspaperman Omar Garrison are perfect companions. The latter presents strikingly drawn faces portraying 67 persons whose lives Jesus touched. Each is accompanied by a short description of the character and the significance of his role in religious history. The result is startling in its realism, beauty and emotional impact. This unique book was a Guideposts Selection in 1958 and completely sold out.

The First Easter represents the very best of Peter Marshall's brilliant talent for speaking and writing. Very few have been so blessed that they could take a portion of Scripture, visualize it in their minds and then describe it in such vivid terms that the scene became moving, real, alive. Peter Marshall was one of those memorable people.

Peter Marshall knew full well that in dealing with the account of the Resurrection, he was reporting on the most crucial portion of the New Testament, for the whole validity of Christianity pivots on its veracity. Either Christ did or did not arise from the dead. Peter Marshall, like a lawyer gathering his facts, has done more than just describe that famous history-changing morning. He has turned the events of that day, the people—Jesus, Simon Peter, Judas, Pilate, Mary Magdalene—into a flesh and blood drama, and when he is finished his case of faith is clear. Movingly he concludes:

> There is no death to those who have entered into fellowship with Him who emerged from the tomb.
> Because the Resurrection is true, it is the most significant thing in our world today.
> Bringing the Resurrected Christ into our lives, individual and national, is the only hope we have for making a better world.
> "Because I live, ye shall live also."
> That is the glorious message of Easter!

The Editors

PETER MARSHALL

THE FIRST

Edited and with an introduction

by CATHERINE MARSHALL

EASTER

with illustrations by *WILLIAM HOFMANN*

THE FIRST EASTER

Guideposts edition published by arrangement with
McGraw-Hill Book Co., Inc.

ACKNOWLEDGMENTS

I wish to express my deep appreciation to Frances Jane Munsey, my most competent and efficient secretary, for her invaluable assistance throughout the preparation of the manuscript; to Miss Sara Leslie for her help with the design and format of the book; and to Dr. Henry Thomas, who checked the manuscript for Biblical accuracy.

I am also grateful to Fleming H. Revell Company for permission to quote from three sermons that first appeared in *Mr. Jones, Meet the Master* by Peter Marshall.

The sermon material used in this book was prepared only for oral delivery and therefore was not completely annotated. Every effort has been made to find any indebtedness to others and to give proper credit. If any material should still remain unacknowledged, the publisher or I will appreciate information to that effect and will be happy to give the usual credit in all future editions of the book.

C. M.

INTRODUCTION

For me the word "Easter" conjures up a procession of pictures. One of the most vivid is a scene from my Georgia college days. On a particular Easter Sunday, I was one of a group of girls who bumped along for fifteen miles on a slow streetcar to attend the Easter service at the Westminster Presbyterian Church in Atlanta.

In retrospect I can see the almost-square church with its high vaulted ceiling and huge interior stone pillars, packed to the doors. The atmosphere was charged with expectancy, interlaced with the heavy fragrance of Easter lilies. Through open windows crept a soft spring breeze, for spring came early to Georgia. The young man in the pulpit made us see and feel and smell the spring. Even in his pastoral prayer he spoke of balmy air, budding trees, and the songs of birds. And I remember that he referred several times to the azaleas—white, and pink, coral, magenta—and to the fairyland of dogwood blossoms and redbud out Druid Hill's way.

Yet a crowded church at Easter, a whispering spring breeze, and poetic imagery in a prayer would scarcely have been enough to make a lasting impression on a school girl. To this service something extraordinary was added. What had happened in a certain Garden almost two thousand years ago was obviously real to this young preacher, Peter Marshall, and he seemed resolutely eager to make it as real to us who listened.

"What do I mean by a resurrection?" he asked. He made it clear that he did not mean "just the perpetuation of a dead man's ideas or influence."

"This," he said earnestly, "is something we dare not water down by what we call 'spiritualizing' it. It must be so authentic that you and I can *see* it . . .

". . . suddenly, at a given time between sunset and dawn . . . there is a rustling as of the breath of God moving through a garden.

A Man rises up from the cold stone slab where He had been laid. We must see Him as He walks to the threshold of the tomb,
    stands swaying for a moment on wounded feet
and walks out into the dewy garden, alive forevermore.

We must be able to see in mind's eye
    the discarded graveclothes lying there,
    like a glove from which the hand has been removed,
    the fingers of which still retain the shape of the hand—
        lying there,
    collapsed a little, slightly deflated,
    because there was between the rolls of bandages a considerable weight of spices . . .

We must be able to *hear* it—
    catch a whiff of the strange scents that must have drifted back to the Man from that tomb
        of linen and bandages
            of spices—myrrh and aloes—
                and close air and blood. . . ."

We who listened were no longer in Atlanta. We were back in a Garden. What was this strange ability of the man in the pulpit to enlist not just our minds, but our imaginations and even our sensory perceptions? I didn't know. All I knew was that this was a new kind of preaching to me.

And why was this young preacher so anxious to make this resurrection a reality to us? Why was he excited about it? He made the reason quite clear. . . . Because of what had happened on that first Easter, we had a living Lord. We could each have vital communion with Him right then, tell Him our problems, get His help and direction for our lives. Moreover—and here a note of exultation came into the preacher's voice—because we could each prove Christ's aliveness for ourselves by our contact with Him, we could have the proof we needed of life after death. Not a one of us need ever fear death again. That was good news, wasn't it? Then it was important that the good news get out.

We college students walked out of the church that morning aglow with concepts that had gotten through to us for the first time. Nor was the spell broken by the traffic on Ponce de Leon, nor by the rumbling old streetcar with its straw seats that carried us back to Decatur. Not Sunday dinner with chicken and grits, nor a history term paper to be written could break the spell. Else why would I remember the details of that Easter service even now?

I could not have known that my life was to be intertwined for all time with the preacher's, not that I would hear a procession of his Easter services through the years to come. Yet no matter how many I heard—the glow, the excitement, the something special was always there. And apparently not just for me, but for many another.

I had a chance to glimpse another of Peter's Easter services six years later through the eyes of someone else. This time the setting was the New York Avenue Presbyterian Church in Washington, D.C., to which Peter and I had come in the fall of 1937. A young woman's life was changed that morning, and this is the way she describes it:

... It was Easter Sunday—a rainy, dismal day, thoroughly in tune with my spirits. As my friend and I stood in line at the church, I wondered why I was there. I had just about lost any faith I had. . . . My husband "Sandy," a new 2nd Lieutenant in the Air Corps stationed at Langley Field, had been killed in a crash four months before. We had had just one glorious year together. . . .

By the time my friend and I got inside the church, there were no seats left except the steps in the balcony. I've never seen a church so crowded. The service began. The music was lovely, and I felt myself relaxing. Then the man in the pulpit began to speak.

How can I put into words what happened to me in the next few minutes? It was as if the whole crowd melted away, and there was the Lord and I. As Dr. Marshall spoke of the resurrection, the full meaning of it came into my heart for the first time. . . .

And when instead of a benediction, the vast congregation rose and stood silently while the choir over a hundred strong, sang "There Is No Death," I thought that I could not possibly stay in my skin and contain that moment of exultation.

I walked away from the service on air. Out on the sidewalk my friend said, "What in the world has happened to you?"

"Something wonderful, Virginia. The weight is gone. I'm all right now. I can go on living."

But I said nothing more because just in case my new feeling of joy might be a passing emotion, I determined to give it a one year test before I told anyone in detail. Well, the peace that had crept into my aching heart and healed it that morning proved to be lasting. A year later, on Easter Sunday, I wrote Dr. Marshall thanking him for introducing me to the One who had brought joy back into my life. . . .

Peter must have liked that letter, because as he saw it, the function of the church is to introduce people and their needs to Jesus Christ. "That," he was fond of saying, "is the church's business, and it is nothing else."

And why is it so important to make that introduction? Because every human being has needs, faults, complexes. The place to begin solving those problems is within. Yet a man can't change his own nature—or anyone else's. But Christ still can.

Peter Marshall was convinced that "no man can look at Jesus of Nazareth and remain the same." It followed that the purpose at the heart of his preaching was to make sure that we in his congregations really looked at Jesus Christ—saw Him vividly, unforgettably. This is not always easy for those individuals (perhaps in the majority) who find the Bible difficult reading. Therefore the pictorial quality of Peter's preaching was an invaluable aid. Yet one would have thought that with Dr. Marshall's sudden death this ministry would have come to an end.

Not so. The public's reception of the first book of his sermons, *Mr. Jones, Meet the Master,* edited and released after his death, was a surprise to everyone. Material intended for oral presentation is often as dry as dust on the printed page. Publishers regard collections of posthumous sermons as notoriously poor risks. *Mr. Jones* proved the exception. Partially because of the book's unusual format—the sermons printed in Peter's own style, a readable style that looks like blank verse—partially because of the vividness of the material itself, *Mr. Jones* became a best-seller.

Even the title was more significant than I knew at the time. It was almost a prophecy of what the book would mean to people. Their letters poured in. What they revealed was that the central purpose at the heart of Peter Marshall's ministry was living on in uninterrupted fashion. People were still being introduced to the Master, and over and over they verified Peter's conviction that "they could never be the same again."

There was nothing stuffy about the Christianity they found. In fact, it was as exciting as Peter had always found it himself. Joy returned to life. As one enthusiastic teen-age girl put it, ". . . Peter was nearly my idol and would have been if I hadn't seen him step out of the way and let me catch a glimpse of the Saviour. I met Him through Peter Marshall."

In the years since *Mr. Jones, Meet the Master* was released, there has been a steady stream of requests for more of Dr. Marshall's sermon material. When I began seriously to consider what should go into such a book, I thought of the fact that to Peter the compass needle of Christianity pointed inevitably and always to Resurrection morning.

Therefore his best thinking, most careful preparation, and all his gifts for sermonizing he had lavished through the years on his Easter sermons. In those sermons his ability to paint a picture in words, to enable his listeners to see and hear and feel an incident rose to its greatest height. I found in my possession 96 Easter manuscripts from eighteen years and four months of preaching. In re-reading these sermons covering the events of Passion Week, I quickly found myself caught up in drama—sheer drama, engrossing, at times tender, at times terrible—and always and always I found myself moved by Peter's ability to enlist the emotions on the side of faith.

Thus *The First Easter* unfolded itself. My only part in it has been to take from the many sermons Dr. Marshall's re-creation of each scene, as event followed event, and edit the material only where it was necessary to weave it together.

Here then is Easter seen through the eyes and described from the heart of one man.

Catherine Marshall

Washington, D.C.
October 19, 1958

THE FIRST EASTER

What is this mysterious, strange, joyous influence
that seems to permeate everything at this time of the year . . .
that lingers, like a sweet perfume, delicate and clean,
to touch us all with its magic?

It is an intriguing thing . . . intangible, yet real.

We feel it . . .
    sense it . . .
        thrill to it.

There is more to it than bunny rabbits
    and colored eggs
        and gay, new clothes.

Easter is more than a celebration
    because the sap is rising in the trees . . .
        and the bare branches are slipping bright green rings
        on bony fingers . . .
    and blossoms are turning wood and garden into fairyland.

Easter is more than a spring festival.
So far as the church is concerned, the message of Easter
is contained in the declaration
           "Christ is Risen!"

1

Did the Lord really rise from the dead?

    Is it true that He is alive?
        Was that tomb in Jerusalem really empty?
          Can we believe it?
Do we believe it?

Either we are dealing here with flaming truth or the hideous
falsehood of the Christian Gospel.
It is important that we know which.

For if the Resurrection is a fact, then the events that took place
in the city of Jerusalem between the 14th Nisan and the 16th
Nisan in the year 3790 or—as we now record time—between
April 7 and April 9, Anno Domini 30, are the most important
and significant events in history.

What did happen?
Hear that story as it is given us . . .

              *   *   *

It was night.

Outside in the streets of Jerusalem, shadows fled before
a full moon rising over the pinnacles of the temple.
Time was ebbing towards its close—and its beginning—
the cleft that would for the rest of recorded history mark it
              Before Christ . . . After Christ . . .

2

A sinister silence beat in upon the heavy hearts of a group
of twelve men gathered in an Upper Room.
They knew that something dreadful was about to happen
and they were apprehensive.
This was the last night of Jesus' life on earth.
He had looked forward to this occasion—
                    having His own apostles—
              His chosen friends—
          His intimate companions
for three years grouped around Him in the fellowship of the
Last Supper.

He had Himself made the arrangements for the supper.
"Look for a man carrying a pitcher of water," He had told
His disciples.
That in itself would be an unusual thing
     for it was the women who usually carried the water.
The man would lead them to this Upper Room, perhaps in
the home of John Mark's father—a guest room built on the
flat roof of the house.

Pillars supported a roof closed in with curtains, and
the curtains billowed and swung in a cool evening breeze.
A lamp hanging from the ceiling cast flickering light.

The men were reclining on couches around a low
U-shaped table.
At the Master's left was Simon Peter . . . at His right, John.

A quiet voice spoke:

> "With desire I have desired to eat this passover
>   with you before I suffer. . . ."

Bronzed hands took a loaf of bread . . .
     gave thanks for it . . .
          broke it . . .

> "This is my body which is given for you:
>   this do in remembrance of me. . . ."

The Last Supper was to institute a memorial—the loving
desire to be remembered.

Christ relied upon homely symbols—
   a piece of bread,
    a cup of the juice of the lowly grape—
to recall Him to future generations.

8

He knew that we would be in constant danger of
forgetting Him . . .
Therefore He enlisted sense on the side of faith and trusted
to these simple everyday memorials for the recalling
to our treacherous memories of His undying love.

> "This is the blood of the new testament—a new
> agreement—which is shed for many for the
> remission of sins . . .
> Drink ye all of it. . . .

> "But I say unto you, I will not drink henceforth
> of this fruit of the vine, until that day when I drink
> it new with you in my Father's kingdom."

Strange words with which to institute a Sacrament.
What did He mean?
The words that fell from His lips that night are standing
evidence of Christ's own estimate as to where the center of
His work lies—
    We are to remember His death.
Never did He ask that we should commemorate His birth . . .
Not once did He request that any of the wonderful deeds
He performed should be immortalized . . .
Only this—His last and greatest work—
                    the work of redemption.

This was to be His memorial—a cross—to remind us that
God's love for us is a love
    that hate cannot nullify
        and death cannot kill.

Already, days before, He had told His apostles:

> "Behold we go up to Jerusalem . . . the Son of Man
> . . . shall be mocked, and spitefully entreated . . .
> and they shall scourge him, and put him to death;
> and the third day he shall rise again. . . ."

*   *   *

Outside the night was silent, as if all Jerusalem held its breath,
feeling the approach of the storm.
Like sequins, the lights of the city appeared
                    twinkling one by one.
And an indigo sky grew darker and darker.
One by one the city's noises were silenced.
But in the room itself there was noise, for the disciples
were quarreling.

Their argument had started earlier in the day as they had
walked to the supper.
Then they had divided into smaller groups, so as not
to attract too much attention as they gathered for
the evening meal.

Because there were no servants to bathe their feet and because
they had been arguing about who was to be chief among them,
nobody had made any gesture of ceremonial washing.

They had walked past the earthenware pitcher of water at
the door and had taken their places around the table—angry

argumentative

sulking

cross

tired.

We can imagine them stretching out their robes so as to cover
their feet—trying to pretend there was nothing wrong—when
everything was wrong.
They had looked like sulky schoolboys.
Who wanted to stoop to do a slave's work?

Now, during the supper, Jesus rose and took off His
outer garment.
Then He took a towel, girded Himself, poured water into
the basin and began to do the menial thing that not one
of them would do—
He began to wash the disciples' feet.

And He did it because He was the Son of God.

That lowly loving deed expressed in all its loneliness
the glory and humility of His own heart.

Did the Apostle John tell us of this incident so that we might
understand that those who shared the Last Supper with Jesus
of Nazareth were no plaster saints?
These were ordinary men—quite like you and me—
    subject to nerves and temper
        to pettiness and self-centeredness.

13

John makes a very significant statement in telling of this incident. He says:

> "And Jesus, knowing that the Father had given all things into his hands, and that he was come from God, and went to God; he riseth from supper . . . and began . . ."

To reveal His death by signs and miracles? No.
To show His authority by displays of superhuman power? No.
To act like an all-powerful dictator? No, no.

Christ, knowing who He was, having come forth from God, knowing that He was going to God, began to "wash the disciples' feet."

The glory of Christ's life on earth was not the ethereal glory of the supernatural . . .

No—but rather the simple fact that He loved us,
    that He loved unlovely men and women
with a love that goes on loving—and goes on loving—so that nothing can ever defeat it . . .
Nothing can ever break it down.

"Having loved His own which were in the world," adds John, "He loved them unto the end."

Then Christ again took His place at the table.

14

All eyes were upon Him.
And a look like shadows blotting out the sun crossed
the Master's face.

> "Verily I say unto you, that one of you shall
> betray me. . . ."

The apostles were shocked.
Peter blurted out, "Lord, surely it isn't I?"
And one by one they all asked, "Lord, is it I?"

> "He it is, to whom I shall give a sop, when
> I have dipped it."

Judas was sitting second from the Master on the right,
with John between them.
Jesus had known all along that Judas had been plotting.
He knew that Judas had gone to the chief priests some days
before and had offered to help them arrest Him.
For Caiaphas, the High Priest, had long since decided
that this Jesus of Nazareth must be gotten out of the way.

So Christ took a piece of bread and, dipping it in a bowl of
haroseth, handed it to Judas.

And slowly Judas rose to his feet.
He strode towards the stairway, then pausing
with one hand on the heavy curtains, he turned
and faced Christ.

An awful look passed between them—
   sorrow on the face of the Master . . .
      determination, strain, evil on the swarthy face of Judas.
Then he turned and was gone.
The curtains swung behind him.
There was silence.

And John adds, "And it was night. . . ."

*   *   *

The eleven men who were left were very quiet.
The voice of Christ was very soft and low—
tender with farewell.

It was now only a matter of hours until Christ and His
disciples would be separated.
He wished to fill those last hours of fellowship with the
tenderest and most significant of His teachings.

The most sacred
   the most tender
      the most heart-felt emotions
are those expressed at the end of the letter . . .

The tenderest caress comes just before the parting.
The softest word just before the conversation is ended,
                      before the train pulls out,
                   before we turn away.

16

We seem to catch the quiet intimacy of that fellowship.
Unforgettable words of parting and comfort were spoken
by Jesus to His friends.
Jesus has written them out for us:

> "Little children . . . a new commandment I give
> unto you, that ye love one another; as I have loved
> you. . . . By this shall all men know that ye are
> my disciples. . . .

> "Let not your heart be troubled; . . . In my Father's
> house are many mansions; if it were not so, I would
> have told you. . . .

> "I will not leave you comfortless. I will come to
> you . . .

> "I am the vine, ye are the branches. . . . Abide in me,
> and I in you. . . .

> "These things I have spoken unto you that in me
> ye might have peace. In the world you have
> tribulation: but be of good cheer; I have overcome
> the world. . . ."

Overcome the world? When the One who spoke was so soon
to fall under the power of Caesar?

Yes, for in reality we must remember that Jesus could have
escaped the cross.
No one compelled Him to go to Jerusalem on that last journey.
Indeed, His friends and apostles urged Him not to go.

17

Watch Him, in the bitter hours that lie immediately ahead,
time after time taking the initiative in deciding His own fate.

Christ had begun His ministry by telling His apostles that the
Son of Man must suffer many things.
Must—there was no other way.
It was for that purpose that He had come into the world.

> "For as Moses lifted up the serpent in the wilderness,
> even so must the Son of Man be lifted up. . . . that
> whosoever believeth in him should not perish but
> have everlasting life."

There was Light in the little room that night.
But beyond the light lay a death-ridden world . . .
in the midst of the military might that was Rome
where life was cheap . . .
in the philosopher's porticoes of Athens
where the mind found no hope . . .
in the dangerous living of the great shipping centers of Asia
Minor to the disease-infested alleys of old Jerusalem—
Men feared death, dodged its hideous grasp, could nowhere
find respite from their fear.

But here was something new . . .
Here was One facing death—not afraid, but confident . . .
already triumphant . . .
already speaking about seeing his friends again . . . about
never leaving them . . .

18

Strange words . . . about being with them to the uttermost
parts of the earth and to the end of time.

How? Why? Because He alone knew the Father's eternal
purpose for what it was—the determination once and for all
to destroy the power of death—
once and for all to deliver men from their lifelong bondage to
the fear of death.

Within a matter of hours, Christ Himself was to become the
instrument by which the Father would—for all time—make
death not a wall . . . but a door.

*   *   *

The Last Supper was over.
And when they had sung a hymn, they went out into the
dark and deserted streets.
It was almost midnight.
Past the Lower Pool and through the Fountain Gate
they walked slowly, moving in little silent clusters.
For a time the narrow cobblestone street, banked high in
the middle, led beside the Brook Kedron.

The group moved up the hill
towards their favorite rendezvous—
                    a garden called Gethsemane.

Here in the deep shadows of the night, moving along in the deeper shadows of the trees, they halted.
A few lights twinkled on the hill opposite, but most of the city was asleep, for it was now after midnight.
They could see the temple, its spire tipped with gold, glistening in the moonlight.
And from the ramparts of the Fortress Antonia they could hear a Roman sentry calling his watch.

As they stood there looking across the valley at the Holy City, they wondered at the strange turn events had taken.
They remembered the re-echoing shouts of the people . . .
the glad Hosannas . . .
and the crown that had been refused.
Some of them were thinking of how Judas had left their fellowship to move out into the darkness.
They were wondering where he was and what he was doing.

The eleven could not know that the betrayer had already agreed to Caiaphas' offer of thirty pieces of silver—
    the cost of a slave, it was—
Or that Caiaphas was even then moving under cover of the velvet night to seek audience with the Roman procurator . . .

> "If the Nazarene is captured this night, will you
> agree to sit in the Tribunal to condemn him
> on the morrow?"

*   *   *

The group moved on into the garden under the gnarled
old trees.
The odor of the olive presses clung to the still night air.

And now there was a period of waiting, as though the Master
deliberately waited for some rendezvous with destiny—
His apostles knew not what.

Once again He could easily have escaped; yet He did not.
There was plenty of time, so much time that the weary
apostles—propped against the olive trees—fell asleep.

While they slept, Christ prayed . . .
    kneeling under the little gray-green leaves that gleamed
    white where the moonlight filtered thróugh.
Was there then no way, no other way? . . .

        "Father, all things are possible unto Thee; take away
            this cup from me . . . ."

"This cup" . . .
Often Christ had seen the bodies of the crucified hanging on
the hill outside the Gennath Gate . . .
Sometimes He had heard their moans and their curses,
seen them writhing in their final agony.

Jesus of Nazareth was a man—a real man.
Every bit of His manhood shrank from such an end.

21

And Luke tells us:

> ". . . being in agony he prayed more earnestly:
> and his sweat was as it were great drops of blood
> falling down to the ground. . . ."

Already He was living the pain of it.
Could ultimate triumph come in no other way?
Human sin—man fleeing God—was capable of dreadful deeds.
Of course . . . But must He be the One to taste every depth
that sin could devise . . .
>   misunderstanding
>   betrayal
>   desertion by friends
>   expediency
> weakness
>   callousness
>   deliberate cruelty
>   excruciating pain
>   death itself . . .
in order to prove finally and forever that no evil is any match
for the Father?

The worn face glistening with sweat—so young in time—
    grown so old in understanding . . .
        bowed in final surrender . . .

> "Nevertheless not what I will, but what Thou wilt."

*   *   *

The stillness of the garden was suddenly broken by the low
sound of voices . . .
And now a flickering torch came into view . . .

and another
and another.

Surely this was a procession.
There were soldiers . . .
Twigs crackled under their feet and they stooped low as they
passed under the olive trees.
Someone in front carried a swinging lantern.

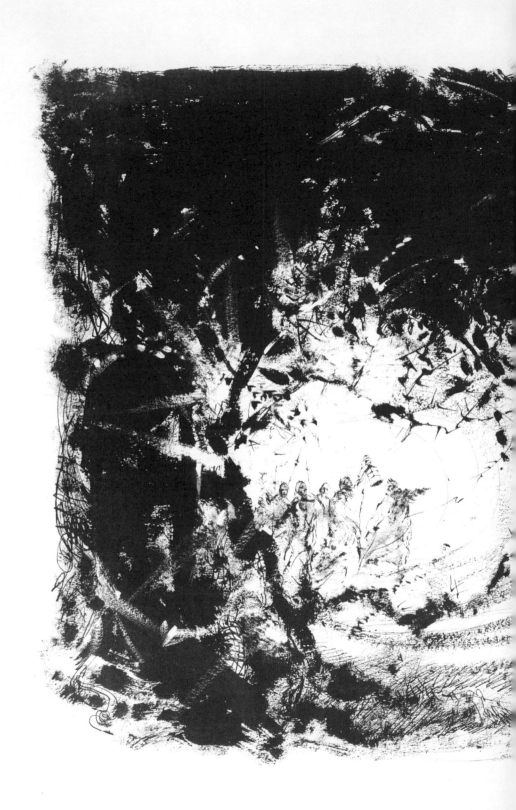

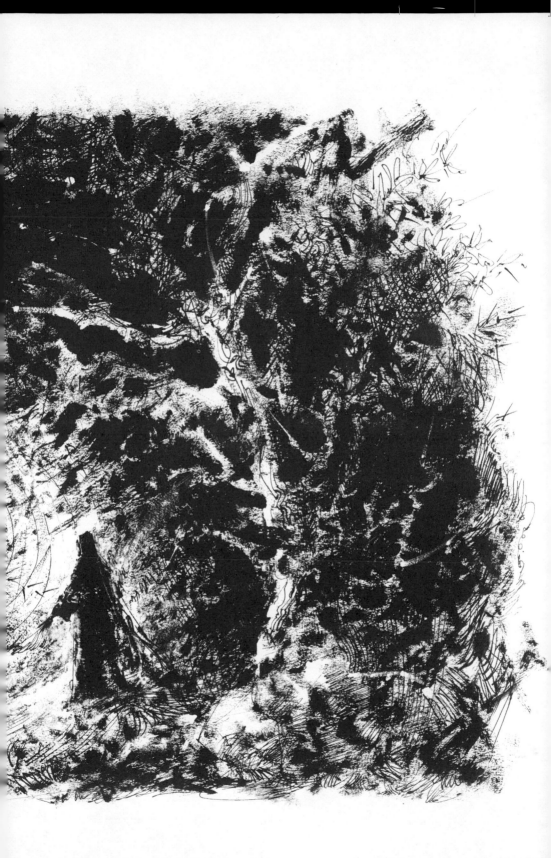

A nondescript mob it was—a rabble of indiscriminate
ruffians—the hangers-on of the temple . . .
        soldiers
       temple guards
      temple doorkeepers
     little priests with big ambitions . . .
who had laid aside their rings of heavy keys . . .
exchanged their brooms for staves and spears and bludgeons—
armed to the teeth, determined to capture the most peaceable
One who ever walked upon the earth.

Out of that sickening crowd there stepped a familiar figure.
It was Judas, a smile upon his face.
"Hail, Master," he said . . . and kissed Him with a kiss that
must have burned Christ's cheek.

Thus identified, Christ was seized . . .
        bound with ropes . . .
      His hands manacled
    His arms tied to His side.

The disciples too were caught in the trap.
After a moment's hesitation, some of them seemed to gain
courage, to think of fighting in defense of their Master.

One asked, "Lord, shall we smite with the sword?"
And Peter—not waiting for the answer—drew from the folds
of his cloak a short sword . . .
   more like a dagger . . .
and recklessly struck a vicious blow at the nearest enemy.

It happened to be the High Priest's servant, whose name was
Malchus—and the blow severed his right ear.

But when Christ saw what Peter had done, he quickly
commanded him to put up his sword:
   "They that take the sword shall perish with the sword."

The method of Peter was the sword . . .
The method of Christ was a cross . . .
Peter sought revenge . . .
Christ sought reconciliation.

Peter cried, "Give me a sword, and we can advance
the Kingdom."
Christ cried, "Give me a cross, and I, if I be lifted up, will
draw all men unto me."

And so they led Him away as a butcher might drag a steer
to the slaughterhouse.

Simon Peter had seen the last flickering torch disappear
round the turn of the path that wound down the hill . . .
Only once in a while could the lights of the procession be seen
through the trees—like giant fireflies.

The murmur of voices died away,
   the crackling of twigs
      and the rustling of dislodged stones through the grass.
There swept over Peter the realization that his Master had at
last been captured and was marching away to die.

The icy fear that gripped his heart was a startling contrast to the flaming courage with which he had drawn his short sword a few minutes before, for this was a different Peter.

He realized that he had blundered, and that he had been rebuked.

Disappointed and puzzled, he could not understand the calm submission with which Christ had permitted them to bind His hands and march Him off.

Realizing that he stood alone in the deserted garden, Peter stumbled blindly down the trail, heedless of the twigs that lashed his face and tore at his robes.

Stumbling on down the hill, instinctively hurrying to catch up with the others, and yet not anxious to get too close, he followed down to the foot of the Mount of Olives, across the Brook Kedron, and back up the hill to old Jerusalem, still asleep and quiet.

The procession made first for the house of Annas, into which they escorted Jesus.

The heavy door creaked shut behind Him, and when Peter approached timidly, it was to find John standing there.

John persuaded the girl stationed at the door to let them in and, as they slipped past her, she scrutinized Peter and said to him:

"Art not thou also one of this Man's disciples?
He said, "I am not."

Perhaps she felt that she could speak to Peter.
Perhaps she felt sorry for him, seeing the hurt, wounded
look in his eyes and the pain in his face.

Who knows what was in her mind?
Perhaps she had seen the Master as they led Him in and felt
the irresistible attraction of the Great Galilean.

Perhaps in that brief moment, as they had crowded past her,
He had looked at her.
If He had—then something may have happened to her,
within her own heart.
Her faith might have been born,
A fire kindled by the spark the winds of strange circumstances
had blown from the altar fires in the heart of the Son of God.

Perhaps she wanted to ask Peter more about the Master.
Perhaps she would have said—had Peter acknowledged Him:
      "Tell me the sound of His voice.
        Is it low and sweet, vibrant?
        Tell me of some of His miracles.
        Tell me how you are sure He is the Messiah.
        What is this salvation He speaks about?
        How can we live forever?"

Maybe these questions would have come tumbling in a torrent
from her lips . . . who knows?

But whatever she meant, whatever her motive for asking
the question,

30

"Art not thou also one of this Man's disciples?"
Peter denied his Lord and said: "I am not."

We can only stand aghast at Peter and wonder if the strain
and the shock have destroyed his memory.

Simon, surely you remember the first day you saw Him.
   Andrew and yourself floating the folded net . . . His shadow
   falling across you as you worked.
Don't you remember His command, His beckoning finger, the
light in His eyes, as He said: "Follow me, and *I will make you
fishers of men"?*

Peter, don't you remember?

And that night when Nicodemus came into the garden
looking for the Master . . .
Don't you remember how he crept in with his cloak pulled
up over his face?

Don't you remember how he frightened you, and how the
Lord and Nicodemus talked for hours about the promises?
Don't you remember the wedding in Cana where He turned
the water into wine?
Don't you remember the music of His laugh and the Samaritan
woman at Sychar?
Don't you remember these things, Simon? . . .

And now they brought the Lord from Annas to Caiaphas, and
the soldiers and the temple guards mingled with the servants
in the courtyard.

Because the night was cold, they had kindled a fire in the brazier, and Peter joined himself to the group and,
stretching out his hands, warmed himself at their fire.

Peter was glad to join the hangers-on huddled around the blaze, for the morning air bit sharply, and he found himself shivering . . .
It was a kindly glow of warmth.

Coarse laughter greeted every joke and they discussed the things such people talk about:
    the prowess of the garrison's chariot drivers
        the gambling losses of their friends
           the new actor from Antioch at Herod's court
               the additional water tax just levied
                  the latest gossip from Rome.

Peter was not paying much attention to their conversation until one of the soldiers nudged him and said:
    "Thou art also of them."
And Peter said, for the second time: "Man, *I am not.*"

Peter, you must remember . . . surely . . . it must be that you are afraid.

Your brave heart must have turned to water.
Surely you cannot have forgotten . . .
Many a time . . . crossing the lake in boats like your own,
    with its high seats,
        its patched sails slanting in the sun,
           and its thick oars?

32

Remember the night He came walking on the water, and you
tried it, and were walking like the Master, until your courage
left you . . . your faith gave way?

Simon, has your courage left you again?

Have you forgotten the pool at Bethesda and how you laughed
when the impotent man rose . . . rolled up his bed
     threw it over his shoulder
          and went away leaping in the air and shouting?

Ah, Simon, you spoke so bravely . . . and now here you are.

For the next hour or so they merely waited.
What was keeping them so long?
They little knew the difficulty of getting witnesses to agree.
They little knew that sleepless men, with tempers raw and
irritated, were trying to find some reason they could submit
to Pilate that would justify their demands for the death
of Jesus.

After an hour had passed, there joined the group a soldier
who had come out of the palace.
As he greeted his friends in the circle, his eye fell on Peter.
He scrutinized him very carefully, and Peter, feeling the
examination of the newcomer, looked around as the soldier
asked: "Did not I see thee in the garden with him?"

One of his friends joined in:
     "Certainly—he's one of the Galileans.
          Just listen to his accent."

And the soldier stubbornly went on: "I am sure I saw him in the garden, for my kinsman, Malchus, was wounded by one of them who drew a sword . . .
And if I am not mistaken—it was this fellow here."

Then Peter, beginning to curse and to swear, said:
  "I know not the man."

He used language he had not used for years.
It was vile . . . even the soldiers were shocked.
They all looked at him in amazement.

They did not appear to notice the shuffling of feet, as soldiers led Christ from Caiaphas to Pilate.
Perhaps they did not make much noise.
They were tired, worn with argument and talk, so they were very quiet.

The group standing round the fire was silent, shocked at the vehemence and the profanity of Peter's denial.
It was a torrent of foulness, but it was his face that startled them.
It was livid
        distorted
     eyes blazing
   mouth snarling like a cornered animal.
It was not a pleasant sight, and they kept silent.
It was a silence so intense that the crowing of a distant cock was like a bugle call . . .

  34

Immediately, Peter remembered the Lord's prophecy:

"Before the cock crow twice, thou shalt deny me thrice."
Like a wave there swept over him the realization of what he
had done.
All of a sudden he remembered what Jesus had said and, with
tears streaming down his face, he turned away from the fire.

Through a mist of tears he saw ahead of him the stairway
that led to Pilate's palace . . .
And by a terrible Providence, it was just at that moment that
Christ was being led up the stairs to appear before Pilate.

The Lord had heard!
The Lord had heard every hot searing word . . .
The Lord had heard the blistering denial . . . the foul,
     fisherman's oaths . . .
He—He had heard it all!

Christ paused on the stair, and looked down over the rail—
     looked right into the very soul of Peter.
The eyes of the two met . . . at that awful moment.

Through his tears all else was a blur to Peter.
But that one face shone through the tears . . .
     that lovely face
          that terrible face
               those eyes—sad, reproachful, tender . . . as if they
               understood and forgave.

Ah, how well he knew Him, and how much he loved Him.

The world seemed to stand still, as for that terrible moment,
Peter looked at the One he had denied.
We shall never know what passed between them.
Christ seemed to say again:

> "But I have prayed for thee, Simon,
>   Satan hath desired to have thee,
>   But I have prayed for thee."

Simon's tears now overflowed and ran down his cheeks—
            hot and scalding tears they were—
And with great sobs shaking his strong frame, he spun round
and rushed out to where the cool morning air might fan his
burning cheeks.

He fled with his heart pounding in his breast, while the
Nazarene walked steadily to meet the Roman governor.

*   *   *

> "Then assembled together the chief priests, and the
> scribes, and the elders of the people, unto the palace
> of the High Priest, who was called Caiaphas,
> And consulted that they might take Jesus by subtilty,
> and kill him.

> "But they said, Not on the feast day, lest there be an
> uproar among the people . . ."

Why did the religionists of Jesus' time want to kill Him?
Why was Caiaphas in particular anxious to get Him out of
the way?
What was the charge against the Nazarene?

The Sadducees were the religious élite of the day.
Not only was Caiaphas, the present High Priest, a Sadducee,
but he was also the son-in-law of Annas, now an old man,
whom he had succeeded in that office.
Now that Palestine was under Roman jurisdiction,
even the High Priest was a Roman appointee.
But so crafty a politician was Annas that Caiaphas was the
seventh member of his own family to receive the coveted
appointment.

Both were wealthy men.
The temple—the religious domain over which they presided—
was also a financial empire.
By a rare financial strategy, they had made it so.

Annas and Caiaphas controlled the market in the temple
porch, where sacrifices were sold to pilgrim worshipers and
Roman money was exchanged for the statutory half-shekel
required as a temple offering.

The priests determined the rate of exchange and made
money shamelessly.

Moreover, they drew rent from the ground on which the sellers of animals for sacrifice put up their stalls and stacked their dove cages.

The people knew this and resented it, but what could they do? What can the general populace ever do about taxes that eat up the fat of the land?

An income equivalent to about a million and a half dollars a year was flowing into the temple treasuries.

Jesus knew all this; it was common knowledge.

No wonder His indignation was aroused, especially when this evil was carried on in the name of worship of the living God.

The most scathing words He ever uttered were spoken against the men who perpetrated this wholesale theft.

The scathing words had come to the ears of Annas and Caiaphas.

For many months they had had spies reporting back to them on the itinerant preacher.

Exactly how dangerous was He?

The day came when the Nazarene strode into the temple court and overthrew the tables of the money changers.

That dynamic figure had stridden about among the merchants, unafraid.

The folds of His robe falling away from His right arm had revealed powerful muscles.

Angry priests had stood helplessly by,
     muttering threats in throaty growls . . .

38

The money changers had screamed in frenzy
     as they had groveled among the filth to retrieve their coins
     that had rolled in a hundred directions.
And the pilgrims who had been bled white all these years had
laughed and added their own shouts of encouragement.

Minutes later an observer had run to tell the servant of
the High Priest.

But Caiaphas was afraid of the common people and dared
not intervene.
For the popularity of this Jesus was largely with the
common folk.
Stories of His wonderful works were everywhere.

The beggars in the streets talked of them . . .
They were discussed by the drivers of the caravans at
every stop . . .
And the stories lost nothing in the telling.

It was said that He healed the blind. . . .
There were cripples who had thrown away their crutches . . .
There was a current story about a little girl who had been dead
and had been restored to her father . . .
And now the latest story—
     the one about Lazarus, a prominent citizen, indeed a wealthy
     man of Bethany, being brought back to life . . .

Caiaphas had secretly checked and rechecked.
That task had not been too difficult, because Bethany was
so close.

He had been unable to find anyone to refute the story—

It was so odd!

Enough to make a man uneasy—

With such power and a growing following, anything could happen.

No wonder the chief priests and the Pharisees got together and asked:

> "What shall we do? for this man doeth many miracles.
> If we let him thus alone, all men will believe on him;
> And the Romans shall come and take away both
> our place and nation."

Caiaphas was the one who suggested a solution.
Only the Romans could execute a death sentence.
Surely it was useless to settle for less.
Nothing else would finally silence the Galilean.
Therefore the crux of the problem was to find a charge against
Jesus that would satisfy Roman law.

The High Priest well knew that if the True Messiah should
ever come, there would be two immediate results . . .
   The political supremacy of Rome would be challenged
   by revolt. This would mean Rome's suppression of the
   revolt by violence,
and
   The Messiah, if accepted by the people, would usurp
   Caiaphas' own position and power.

Did not this Jesus claim to be the Messiah?
Then this was the perfect charge . . .
So Caiaphas argued to the priests:
> "It is expedient for you that one man should die for
> the people, and that the whole nation perish not."
> *"From that day forth, they took counsel that they
> might put him to death."*

*   *   *

And now, with Judas' help, it had come.
The Nazarene,
   His hands bound with ropes,
   His face and beard matted with blood from the blows
   of the soldiers . . .
stood before him.

The court had been hastily convened in the middle of the
night.
Some of Caiaphas' colleagues might have been drowsy and
half-asleep at that time, but the High Priest was
thoroughly alert.

For hours he had been busy getting word to the
seventy members of the Sanhedrin . . .
   trying to round up men who would testify against Christ.
Haste was important.

The members of the Sanhedrin sat on stone seats in a
three-tiered semicircle.
Some seats were vacant; it was still an hour before dawn.

Witness after witness came forward.
But the witnesses could not agree among themselves
and the prisoner refused to say anything.
As soon as one spoke against Jesus, another contradicted
and a great tumult broke out.

Caiaphas grew red in the face with mounting frustration.
He had already risked much to bring Jesus to trial:

> It was illegal for the temple guard, acting under the orders
> of the High Priest, to arrest the prisoner.
> The arrest should have been made spontaneously by
> the witnesses.
> It was clearly against the law to try a capital charge
> at night.

Finally Caiaphas, having utterly failed with his witnesses,
knew that nothing that had been said could give the color of
justice to the sentence of death.
He rose from his seat and walked over to where he could
look down into the calm face of the prisoner.
If witnesses could not condemn Him, he must try to get Him
to condemn Himself.

Turning to the Nazarene, the judge addressed Him:

42

"Answerest thou nothing to the things which these
witnesses say against thee?"

But Jesus held His peace.
The silence angered the High Priest.
He seemed ready to explode.
The jewels on his robes sparkled and flashed in the light from
the bronze lamps, as his eyes flashed anger.
And then, with all the authority he could crowd into the words,
Caiaphas put to Jesus the solemn Jewish oath of testimony:

"I adjure thee by the living God . . ."

When a question was put like that to a loyal Jew,
it was an offense not to answer.

Caiaphas was asking a question that really mattered—
a question that required an answer clear-cut, like
chiseled marble—
And the question rang out through the assembly:
"I adjure thee by the living God, that thou tell us
whether thou art the Christ, the Son of God?"

Priests and rabbis,
scribes,
Pharisees and Sadducees,
learned men of Israel . . .
They all knew what the question meant.

They sprang to their feet in the excitement, craning forward
to catch the reply.

Would the Nazarene reply?

If He kept His silence, then the Sanhedrin would have no choice but to release Him.

His life hung on His answer . . .

Once again Jesus took the initiative on His road to the cross.

He would answer!

His voice rang out.

There are three versions of His reply in the Gospels!

Mark writes it: "I am."

   Matthew writes it: "Thou hast said."

      Luke writes it: "Ye say that I am . . ."

The meaning is the same.

There was no doubt in the mind of the High Priest as to what Jesus' reply signified.

At last he had triumphed.

He swung round on the assembled rabbis, tearing his robe from top to bottom, according to custom.

His voice shrill with victory, he shouted:

      "What further need have we of witnesses?"

The charge of blasphemy had been established.

It was sufficient.

The Sanhedrin had no choice but to impose the solemn sentence:

      "He is liable to be put to death."

*   *   *

The Roman Procurator, Pontius Pilate, was not in the best
of moods.
He did not relish having to rise at cockcrow to try a case.
These Jewish people over whom Caesar had sent him to rule
four years earlier were a difficult, turbulent race.
The army of occupation was forever trying to keep the lid
on a smoldering volcano.

Pilate had a soldier's contempt for religion.
Of course, it was true that he was superstitious—
    some unexpected event . . .
    some omen . . .
    a dream . . .
    the pronouncement of some oracle . . .
    the voice of a soothsayer in the marketplace . . .
    the cast of the dice . . .
These could cause him to tremble.
But as for religion . . .
Well, he had seen many religions—
    in Egypt and Persia, through Asia Minor and Macedonia—
And they all seemed alike to him.

No prayers and mystic rites could stand up against
the Roman legions.

As for him, give him a legion of hardy veterans . . .
                    shining armor . . .
                  flashing spears . . .
              trusty swords . . .
And a fig for all the religions in the world!

Yet these religious Jews baffled him—irritated him.
He had tried putting them down by force.
There had been the affair of the money he had taken from the
Sacred Treasury to better Jerusalem's water supply,
and the bloody revolt that had followed.
And that incident of the votive shields
in the Herodian Palace . . .

46

Yes, he had tried riding roughshod over their prejudices.
And the moment he had touched their religion, they had risen defenseless as sheep but as angry as wolves.

It was all so illogical and absurd!
Such may well have been his thoughts as he strode through the outer door of the Praetorium towards this unpleasant early morning hearing.

The Roman paused at the head of the marble staircase. With cool scrutiny he regarded the crowd before him.
On his shaven face with its keen eyes there was just a trace of a sneer, for he had been told that the Jews had ceremonial objections to treading the stones of the Gentile palace lest they be made unclean for the passover.
So he, Pilate, must go out to them.

Grimly, he gathered his purple-bordered toga over his arm and strode down the steps.
The seething mass of humanity before him seemed centered around one solitary Man who was being thrust forward.
Pilate's first impression was that He was perfectly harmless.
He looked Him over with the eyes of a trained soldier.
He looked first for a sign of weapons . . . There was none.

The prisoner was dressed in a simple white robe,
               open at the neck,
                  wrinkled and soiled from rough handling.
His hands were bound behind His back.
Pilate then looked for confederates or friends of the prisoner.
There were none.

47

Many of the faces before him were livid.
The crowd looked like a pack of snarling animals.
The Roman governor raised his baton as a signal that the trial
could begin and asked:
"What accusation bring ye against this man?"

The reply was insolent . . .
"If he were not an evil-doer we should not have delivered him
up to thee."

Once more Pilate looked at the prisoner.
An evil-doer?
If the Roman was any judge of men—
    and he prided himself on that—
this prisoner was no vicious character.

"Take him away," he said, turning to go back into the palace.
"Take him away and deal with him according to
your own law."

Now a veritable howl went up . . .
"It is not lawful for us to put any man to death."

Ah, so that was what they wanted . . .
The blood-lust was in their eyes.
He knew now what the Jews wanted of him—to make conven-
ience of his rank and position . . .
But woe be to him if he blocked their intentions.

Pilate hesitated.
Once more his eyes rested on the prisoner.

His was the only calm face in that seething sea—
                                    and what a face it was!

There was something in the eyes . . .
    in the set of the mouth . . .
        something about the bearing that was different—
                                    strange
                                    compelling.

There came to the Roman governor an instinctive desire to
get away from the crowd,
    to be alone with this Man and speak with Him face to face.

So he turned and strode back into the palace and sat down
upon the dais.
Then he gave command that the prisoner be brought before
him.

Quietly and with stately mien, Jesus—the chiliarch of the
Twelfth Legion beside Him—walked across the mosaic floor
until He stood in front of the powerful Roman, and turned
His deep, searching eyes upon Him.

Outside of the narrow pointed windows the sound of the
impatient murmuring of the crowd was wafted into
the Judgment Hall.
Pilate paid no attention.
His hands rested on the gilded carving of the bisellium.
His eyes narrowed as they stared moodily at the white-robed
figure before Him.

For a moment there was silence.

Then Pilate's involuntary question surprised even himself:

"Art thou the King of the Jews?"

A faint smile came over the face of Jesus . . .

"Sayest thou this of thyself or did others tell it thee concerning me?"

It was the first time that Pilate had heard the Man's voice. He did not say so, but it was the prisoner's deportment that had made him involuntarily associate kingliness with Him.

"Am I a Jew?" he asked contemptuously.

"Thine own nation and the chief priests have delivered thee unto me. Tell me—what hast thou done?"

A faraway look came into the eyes of Christ.

He seemed to be seeing into the far distances.

He had done many things in three short years.

He had never hurried;
yet He had been conscious of time fleeting.
And He had warned His disciples that the night cometh when no man can work.

Yet the seed had been sown.
Eleven men had been impregnated with the Gospel.
The increase would come in due time.
His task was almost finished now.
Only one great act remained, and it was moving swiftly towards its climax.

50

What had He done?

No crime certainly—no political misdemeanor.

Had He not told John's messengers:

> ". . . the blind receive their sight, and the lame walk,
> and the lepers are cleansed, and the deaf hear, and
> the dead are raised up, and the poor have the Gospel
> preached unto them."

That was something . . .

But Pilate would not be interested in that.

So He said gently:

> "My kingdom is not of this world: if my kingdom
> were of this world, then would my servants fight,
> that I should not be delivered to the Jews: but now
> my kingdom is not from hence."

Pilate persisted:

> "Art thou a king then?"

"Anything less like a king—judged by his own standards—
could hardly be imagined," thought Pilate.

The prisoner stood before him alone,

without a single person to plead His cause.

He stood there arrayed in a plain seamless, soiled robe,
    the dress of a peasant.

Here at any rate was no king whom Caesar need fear.

> "My kingdom is not of this world," Jesus had said.

His kingdom did not belong to the same order of things as
Caesar's kingdom.

Therefore, the two could never come into collision.
His kingdom was a repudiation of all political aims.
It was a flat denial of the insinuations made by the priests
that the Nazarene was plotting treason.

But it was an assertion that claimed kingship of some sort . . .
So Pilate probed further . . .

    "So thou art a king then?"

And Jesus nodded.

    "Thou sayest. . . . To this end have I been born,
        that I should bear witness unto the truth. Every one
        that is of the truth heareth my voice."

Pilate seemed a little weary of the interview.
He had learned what he wanted to know—
      this man was harmless.

    "What is truth?" he asked.

Then, without waiting for a reply, he rose and went outside
to give his answer to the impatient Jews.
He held up his baton for silence.
In a ringing voice he said:
    "I find no fault with this man."

The chief priests were now more angry than ever.
They spat out their accusations . . .

    "He stirreth up the people.
      He teacheth throughout all Jewry,
      beginning from Galilee to this place. . . ."

52

The word "Galilee" leaped out at Pilate.
He saw a possible loophole . . .

"Is this man from Galilee?"

When the priests answered in the affirmative, he said firmly:
"Then send the prisoner to Herod.
I cannot try this case. It is not in my jurisdiction."

And Pilate thought that he had dismissed the matter,
was well-rid of an embarrassing issue.
The New Testament narratives leave no doubt that
what Pilate most wanted was to find a way to release Christ.

But Christ before Herod was a greater enigma to the Jewish
ruler than to the Roman.
Herod expected to see Him do some tricks, for the stories
of His miracles had long since been trickling into the court.
The Jewish king was eager for a command performance.

But Jesus stood, silently eloquent.
He had nothing to say—nothing, that is, to Herod.
So Herod sent Him back to Pilate.

The howlings for His death now became even more vehement.
And Pilate, supremely weary now of the whole matter, sat,
chin in hand, on his curule chair—
the cobalt-blue chair of judgment under the
movable canopy—
gloomily watching the yelling mob.

At that moment, a cohort bowed before him.

"Sire, an urgent message . . ."

And he handed the Roman a thin wax tablet.

It was a message from Pilate's wife—Claudia.
Pilate frowned, because never before had Claudia interrupted
him in the midst of a hearing.
Ordinarily, she would have not dared.
The message was the more urgent for its brevity:

> "Have thou nothing to do with that just man:
> for I have suffered many things in a dream
> because of him."

Pilate's thoughts went back to the night before . . .

the nocturnal visit of the High Priest . . .

Claudia had questioned him after the High Priest had left.
Husband and wife had quarreled a bit . . .

> "It isn't really like you—a Roman—to agree
> to a man's death ahead of time.
> I have seen this man in the streets of Jerusalem,
> watched him once for minutes on end from my litter.
> He seems harmless enough. I don't like this affair."

Pilate had slipped out that morning at cockcrow without
waking Claudia—
Now this—the Roman Procurator's hand trembled a bit.
Dreams made him uneasy.
Warnings *could* come that way.
Perhaps Claudia was right after all . . .

54

Pilate leaned forward intently in his chair.

> "Ye have brought this man unto me, as one that
> perverteth the people: and behold, I,
> having examined him before you, have found
> no fault in this man touching those things
> whereof ye accuse him:

> "No, nor yet Herod: for I sent you to him; and lo,
> nothing worthy of death is done unto him.

> "I will therefore chastise him and release him."

But the whole multitude burst into a shout,

> "Away with this man! If you release any,
> release Barabbas."

Pilate shouted, "Barabbas is a robber and a murderer.
What harm has this Jesus done?"

But the mob would not listen.
Prompted by the priests, they shouted, "Crucify . . .
> > crucify . . .
> > crucify . . ."
In a chant that beat with unreasoning insistence and rose
and fell like the waves of an angry sea.

The Procurator could scarcely make himself heard.
He stood outwardly patient,
    his lips curling,
        and an ugly look in his eyes . . .

        "Would you have me crucify your King?"

That enraged them the more . . .

        "We have no King but Caesar."

Desperately Pilate tried once more.
He held up his baton . . .

        "I know it is your custom to have a man released
        at your Festival. There is nothing in this Jesus that
        deserves death. If it will please you, I shall scourge
        him and let him go."

But the mob would not have it so.
Then the voice of Caiaphas rose high and clear
above the clamor:

        "Any man who sets himself up as a King is a rebel
        against Caesar . . . ."

The clear insinuation was, "Do you want me to get word back
to Rome that you have encouraged rebellion against Caesar?"

And now Pilate motioned for Jesus to be brought closer to
the curule chair.
In some strange way this Nazarene had impressed him.

Perhaps it was the look in His eyes.
It was something that made Pilate feel uncomfortable.

Of course the Roman governor had seen many zealots.
He had grown accustomed to them.
Down from the hill country they would bring an insurrec-
    tionist . . . with blazing eyes . . . wild twitching mouth . . .
Or men with pin points of fire for eyes . . .
    and hatred smoldering for the emblems of Rome . . .
Or some poor devils caught in the toils of religious bigotry.
He used to watch them in a detached way with a sneer
in his heart.

But this was different.
He had spoken to this prisoner, and it made him
the more uncertain.

He had a curious feeling that Claudia was right; there was
more in this than met the eye.
Surely he was enough of a politician to find some loophole,
some way to handle this curious case.

He addressed himself to the prisoner:
        "Whence art thou?"

But Jesus only looked at him straight in the eyes and
said nothing.
The silence puzzled Pilate.
The prisoner had talked to him inside the Judgment Hall.
Why not now?

60

"Speakest thou not unto me? Knowest thou not
that I have power to crucify thee, and have power
to release thee?"

It was almost as if Pilate were saying,
"Only say the word, and I shall release thee.
Only tell me that thou art no insurrectionist . . ."
And so, once again, Christ could have escaped the cross—
But He would not . . .

And so Jesus answered—slowly—clearly—

"Thou couldest have no power at all against me,
except it were given thee from above: therefore he
that delivered me unto thee hath the greater sin."

Christ's words did not irritate Pilate.
He squared his shoulders, all the more determined to find
a way to release the Nazarene.

But now the sea of humanity before him
took up the cry again . . .
"Crucify . . ."
"Crucify . . ."
"Crucify . . ."

The tumult was beyond all control, and a guard of soldiers
moved nearer Pilate—just in case—
But he waved them back, and spoke to an attendant who
hurried inside.

61

Pilate stood there waiting, unable to hide his contempt.
The prisoner before him was pale and very tired, swaying a bit
on his feet.
The Roman looked over His head to the priests—
                 seeing the hate in their eyes
              hearing the savagery of their shouting,
and he found himself wondering about their religion . . .
   marveling at any religion that would permit them
   to behave like this.

By this time a servant returned bearing a basin of water and
a towel.
Pilate, unable to make himself heard at all now, wanted to
dramatize something.
Deliberately, in the sight of them all,
   slowly he washed his hands . . .
      slowly dried them.

Now the tumult gradually died.
Then he stepped forward and said clearly and deliberately:
        "I am innocent of the blood of this just man.
          See ye to it!"

And with loud shouts of triumph, the people yelled:
        "His blood be on us and on our children."

Pilate shuddered involuntarily.
He had tried . . . he could tell Claudia he had tried.
Perhaps, by washing his hands, he had dispelled the evil omen.

62

His last act, before turning Jesus over to be scourged and crucified, was to write the inscription to be put over His cross . . .
    in Latin
   in Greek
and in Hebrew:

> "Jesus of Nazareth, King of the Jews."

When Caiaphas saw it, he remonstrated:

> "That is no accusation. People will not understand.
> Do not write 'King of the Jews,' but 'He said I am
> King of the Jews.' "

But Pilate answered bitterly, almost spitting out each word:

> "What I have written I have written."

And from a distant courtyard there came the sound of
a flagellum, into which had been fastened bits of lead and glass
and bone and chain, striking again and again the bared back
of the Nazarene.

*   *   *

The little man Judas had followed the crowd to the courtyard
of the Fortress Antonia.
Slinking, keeping well to the fringe of the screaming mob,
he had watched with mounting horror the sequence of events.
When the farce of a trial had finally reached its climax
and Judas had heard the mob shouting:

> "His blood be on us and on our children"

he had gathered his robes about him, and turned fleeing.

How could he have known it would turn out like this?
He had so hoped that his action would force the Master's hand,
    force Him to go ahead and establish His earthly king-
    dom . . .
But crucifixion? Not *that!*

The thirty pieces of silver in the leather purse dangling
around his waist seemed to be burning his thighs.
This was now blood money.
Somehow, someway he must get rid of it . . .
He raced through the narrow twisting streets towards the
temple, dodging people and donkeys as he went.
Once he almost collided with a man carrying a basket of figs,
and the man swore loudly at his retreating figure.

In the temple he asked a doorkeeper to see the Chief Priest.
"Through that room and along the colonnade to the right,"
the doorkeeper said.
Then, noting Judas' wild eyes, "No, wait—let me see—"
but already the wild one was racing towards the colonnade.

Judas burst into a room where some of the elders
were assembled.
His hands clutched convulsively at the money bag swinging
at his waist.
His eyes were bloodshot.
"I have sinned," he said.

Eyebrows went up; there were questions in the eyes.
The elders noted that this strange man was panting.

"I have sinned in that I have betrayed innocent blood . . .
You know—Jesus of Nazareth. He had done nothing amiss . . .
I did not know that . . ."

Shoulders shrugged.
Sardonic smiles appeared on some of the faces.
 "Jesus of Nazareth? Oh, yes—that one.
Well—what is that to us? See thou to that . . ."

Judas could not believe what he had just heard.
Then the truth dawned on him . . .
The fate of Christ was already out of the hands of these men;
moreover they didn't *care* . . .
The Master was going to die after all . . .
There was nothing he could do about it . . .

With trembling hands he seized the coin purse and opened it.
Slowly he counted out thirty pieces of silver.
Once again he looked questioningly into the eyes of the elders
standing before him.
He saw only amusement—
With a contemptuous gesture Judas flung the silver at them
                              right into their faces.
They ducked the shower of silver, and the coins fell to the
marble floor, rolling in all directions.
Then Judas turned and fled from the room.

The little man did not stop running until he was outside
the city gates.
A picture kept flashing before his eyes—he brushed his hands
before his eyes but it would not leave.
It was Jesus' face at that moment when he, Judas, had
kissed His cheek.

"Friend," He had said gently, "wherefore art thou come?
Why have you done this?"

"Friend," that was what He had said. "Friend"—why have you done this?

   It broke Judas' heart . . .

His plan had failed.
Everything was smashed . . . his dreams . . . his hopes . . .
        his life—everything.
There was nothing left—now.
Only one way out . . .

A few hours later the body of Judas was found
swinging crazily from the branch of a tree on the precipitous
heights overlooking the Valley of the Hinnom.
He had died before the Master.

    *   *   *

An orange morning sun was rising higher and higher over
the City of David.
Pilgrims and visitors for the Feast were pouring in through
the gates, mingling with merchants from the villages round-
about,
   shepherds coming in from the hills,
  hucksters leading their laden camels in single file,
 donkeys standing sleepily beneath their burdens in the
dappled sunlight.

The narrow streets were crowded.
There were the aged, stooped with years, muttering to
themselves as they pushed through the throngs.
There were children playing in the streets, calling to each
other in shrill voices.

And beggars raising sightless sockets to the sky,
                    tapping sticks on the cobblestones
                    demanding alms in nasal voices.

From every balcony and latticed window came
                    the sound of voices
                scraps of laughter
            rude voices, bargaining.

There were men and women carrying burdens . . .
                    baskets of vegetables
                    of green almonds and sweet lemons
                casks of wine
            water bags.

There were cloth merchants with their bales.
Fruiterers were arranging their stalls in narrow bazaars
striped with sunlight.
Tradesmen with their tools seemed out of place in the
holiday atmosphere.

It was not easy to make one's way through the crowd.

70

It was especially difficult for the procession that started out from the governor's palace.

At its head rode Longenius, the Roman centurion in charge of a half maniple of the famous Twelfth Legion.
He seemed a typical Roman, scornful alike of child or cripple who might be in his way.

Before him went two legionnaires, one of them carrying a board atop a pole on which had been printed the charges against those to be executed.
The legionnaires were clearing the crowd aside as best they could, with curses and careless blows.

The procession moved at a snail's pace.
The soldiers tried to keep step.
The centurion's guard evidently did not relish this routine task, which came to them every now and then in the governing of this troublesome province.

The sunlight glanced on the spears and helmets
of the soldiers.
There was a clanking of steel as their shields touched their belt buckles and the scabbards of their swords.
Between the two files of soldiers staggered three condemned men, each carrying a heavy bar of wood with its crosspiece, on which he was to be executed.

It was hard to keep step, for the pace was slow, and the soldiers were impatient to get it over.

Left . . . right . . . left . . . right . . .

In sharped clipped commands they urged their prisoners on.

The crosses were heavy, and the first of the victims was at the point of collapse.

He had been under severe strain for several days.

He had eaten little and had not closed His eyes for two days.

Moreover, the lashing with the flagellum had taken the last bit of His strength.

The carpenter followed them, with his ladder and his nails, and they all moved forward out of the courtyard of Pilate's palace towards the Gennath Gate.

The orange sun was hot.

The sweat poured down the face of Jesus, and He swayed now and then under the weight of the cross.

A depression had fallen on the soldiers, and they marched in silence, as if reluctantly.

A group of women went with the procession, their faces half-hidden by their veils, but their grief could not be hidden.

Some were sobbing . . .

    Others were praying . . .

        Others were moaning in that deep grief that knows not what it says or does.

72

Some of them had children by the hand and kept saying over
and over . . .
   "He gave my child back to me . . .
   How can they be so cruel?
   I know He healed my child—
   What harm could there be in that?"

And there were men, too, who followed as closely as they
could—men who walked with the strange steps of those to
whom walking was unfamiliar.
They were the cripples He had healed.

Others carried sticks in their hands—sticks that once
had tapped out their blind tattoo along the city streets and
the sun-hardened trails of Judea.

They did not use their sticks now, although once again they
were blind . . . blinded by tears.

Once when the procession halted for a moment, Jesus turned
and spoke to them, but they could not hear Him for the
shouting of the rabble.

Most of the crowd hardly knew what was going on.
They did not understand.
They caught the infection of the mob spirit.

They shouted to the first of three victims.
That one had an absurd crown on His head,
    twisted from a branch of the long-thorned briar.
It had lacerated His scalp and caused blood to mingle
with the sweat.

They shouted at Him, until roughly pushed aside by the
soldiers, and then, in some cases, they began to shout at
the soldiers.
It was an ugly situation as the procession went slowly along
this way that will forever be known as the Via Dolorosa.

Meanwhile—Simon of Cyrene was approaching the city gate.

He had just arrived in Judea, and was about to enter the
Holy City, as a pilgrim for the festival.
He had spent the night in some village just outside, and,
rising early that morning, had bathed and dressed himself
carefully . . . with a tingling excitement because soon he
would be in Jerusalem.

The wonders of Jerusalem, that exiles had described, he
would now see with his own eyes.
The sounds of the Holy City which lonely hearts heard in
their nostalgia . . .
    Noises that seemed to be whispered by the restless surf of
    distant seas, or heard in the moaning of winds that
    traveled far . . .
These he would hear with his own ears.

74

Yet he tried to keep calm, and as he set out on the short walk that lay between him and the city, he was very thoughtful.

He walked along the winding path that sometimes ran through the fields . . .

> sometimes along narrow roads between hedges where
> there was the fragrance of pomegranate trees
> and honeysuckle . . .
>
> sometimes along the tortuous course of the dried-up river
> bed where the earth was cracked with the heat
> of the sun.

Sometimes it wound up the jagged hillside to twist down among the giant boulders and huge rocks behind which many a robber might hide.

He walked along beside the tall rushes, where he frightened coveys of birds that flew wheeling, diving . . .

And he walked through the divided crops, ripening in the sunshine.

He could hear the sheep bleating on the inhospitable hillside, while the morning sun climbed higher and chased away the mists that lay in the hollows, trailing down into the ravines like tulle scarves.

As he walked along, he was thinking of the temple and its glories, the history of his people and the worship of his fathers . . .

Already he could see ahead of him the domes of the temple gleaming gold in the sunshine, could hear the pigeons that had their nests in the cupolas and gables,

And he thought of his own city looking from her height over
the blue waters of the Mediterranean.

Then as he neared the city gate he began to hear shouting
that grew louder and louder.
There seemed to Simon to be a sort of chant running through
the noise . . .
    a refrain that men's voices made clearer and clearer
until he thought he could recognize the word
      "Crucify
     crucify
      crucify . . ."
They met right at the city gate . . . Simon of Cyrene and
the crowd.

He found that the procession was headed by some Roman
soldiers; he would recognize them anywhere . . .
    the insignia on their shields . . .
   and their uniforms . . .
He could tell a legionnaire when he saw one.

He had little time to gather impressions, and as for asking
questions, that was impossible.
He could not make himself heard in all the rabble.
The noise and confusion with its sinister and malice made
Simon shudder.
Simon was aware of two moving walls of Roman steel.

There was something strange about it all but, before he could understand it, Simon was caught up in it—sucked into the procession, and swept out through the gate again.

Simon was excited, afraid . . .
He was puzzled and ill at ease.
He scanned face after face quickly, looking for some light
of pity . . .
    of friendliness,
       of welcome . . .
But he found none.

He felt the drama of the situation, the cruelty of it . . .
And its horror crept over him like a clammy mist—
and he shivered.

He was captured by the procession, stumbling along
tightly wedged in the very heart of the crowd.
Then he noticed that there were three men who staggered
under the weight of crosses of rough, heavy wood on which
these unfortunates were going to die.

Each man was bent beneath the burden he carried, and
perspiration moistened his drawn face.
One of them was strangely appealing, His face was arresting.
Simon felt his gaze returning again and again to that one face.
He noticed that blood was trickling down from wounds
in the brow.

On His face there was a twig of long-thorned briar, twisted
around in the shape of a crown and pushed down cruelly
on His head.

Simon watched with beating heart as they shuffled along,
fascinated by the look in those eyes.
He could see nothing else.
Everything was forgotten, even why he had come to Jerusalem.

This public execution had driven everything else from
his mind.
Forgotten for the moment were the temple and its services,
    messages he brought from friends far away . . .
        things he had been asked to get . . .
Everything was forgotten as he watched this Man carrying
the cross.

And then *He* looked up! His eyes almost blinded by the blood
that trickled down from under that grotesque crown that was
on his head . . .
Why didn't somebody wipe His eyes?

And as Simon looked at Him, He looked at Simon . . .
And the eyes of the two . . . met!
How did Christ know what was in Simon's heart?
What was it that made Him smile, a slow, sad smile that
seemed to still Simon's wildly beating heart and give
 him courage?

The look that passed between them Simon never forgot as long as he lived, for no man can look at Jesus of Nazareth and remain the same.

As these two looked at each other, the Man with the cross stumbled, and the soldiers, moved more by impatience than pity, seeing that the Nazarene was almost too exhausted to carry the cross any further, laid hands on Simon and conscripted him to carry it.

He was the nearest man.
He was strong.
His shoulders were broad!

Simon's heart almost stopped beating; he tried to speak, but no words came.
A few minutes before, he had been a lonely pilgrim quietly approaching the Holy City.
And now, there he was in the midst of a procession of howling men and women, walking between two moving walls of Roman steel, and carrying on his shoulder a cross on which someone was going to die!

The look of gratitude and love that flashed from the eyes of Jesus as Simon lifted the load from those tired, bleeding shoulders did something to the man from Cyrene, and in an instant life was changed.

Simon never could explain it afterwards—how it happened!

There are moments of spiritual insight that defy the limits
of syntax and grammar.
There are experiences that can never be poured into the
moulds of speech.
There are some things too deep for words.

But all at once he saw the meaning of pain . . .
    understood the significance of suffering . . .
The meaning of prayer was unveiled . . .
    and the message of the Scriptures.
He saw prophecy take form and live before him.
He remembered words of the psalmist and the prophets of old,
words that until now had been without sense or meaning,
but now . . . he saw . . . and understood.

*   *   *

And so the crowd came to Golgotha, a hill shaped like a
skull, outside the city gates, where two great highways, the
Samaria-Jerusalem road and the Joppa-Jerusalem road,
converged upon the city.

Only as the nails were driven in, did the shouting stop.
There was a hush.
    Most of them were stunned . . . horrified . . .
Even the hardest of them were silenced.

Mary, the mother of Jesus, closed her eyes and stopped her
ears; she could not bear the thud of the hammer.

Simon of Cyrene from time to time wiped away his tears with
the back of his hand.
Peter stood on the fringe of the crowd, blinded by hot tears
that filled his eyes, while his very heart broke.

A group of soldiers took hold of the crossbeam and lifted it
slowly off the ground.
With each movement the nails tore at the shredded flesh in
the wrists of the Nazarene.
The cross swayed in the air for a moment and then with a thud
dropped into the hole prepared for it.

When the first spasm of pain had waned, Jesus opened
His eyes.
Over the heads of the crowd, He could see the city,
tawny-yellow, like a crouching tiger in the mid-day sun.

Nearer there was a hillside carpeted with anemone
and cyclamen.
For just a moment a gentle spring wind blowing across the
face of the suffering Man blew away the smell of blood and
wafted to Him the fragrance of flowers, and He saw a single
lark circling high above the hillside.

But closer still a mad medley of fury surged below Him . . .
There were eyes watching this Man on His cross . . .
    unbelieving eyes
        eyes with gloating in them
            other eyes that looked and never saw.

Faces were looking up at Him . . . convulsed faces
     snarling, invective faces,
faces that through His pain-glazed eyes seemed to melt
and run together.

Fingers pointed up to Him hanging quivering on the
cross-gibbet . . .
     long bony fingers . . .
         mocking, accusing fingers—fingers of scorn and ridicule.

There was noise . . . confused noise that beat upon His ears
with an added pain.
There was demoniac laughter that enjoyed suffering.
There was hoarse shouting that taunted and mocked.

From one side of Him there were sighs of pain and the soft
moans of a dying thief, and on the other side blasphemies and
curses terrible to hear.
There was weeping too, the crying of the women and the
unashamed sobbing of men.

The wounded flower of Magdala was consoled by that lovely
one who had once held Him in her arms, while the beloved
John stood beside them.

The crowd hurled His own words back at Him, but they were
barbs, dipped in venom and shot from snarling lips, like
poisoned arrows.

     "He saved others, himself he cannot save.
       Yes, he healed the cripples.

82

Yes, he gave sight to the blind.
He even brought back the dead, but he cannot
save himself."

They were willing now to grant the truth of His miracles.
Out of the mouths of His enemies comes this testimony to His
power—"He saved others" . . .

Yes, they were saved—those others . . .
  saved from the land of shadows
    saved from the caves of derangement
      from the couches of pain
      from the leprous touch of sickness
    saved from the enslaving grip of vice
  saved even from the jaws of death.
Yes, He had saved others—His enemies admitted it . . .

But now their taunt rose to its crescendo—

> "Perform a miracle now, Miracle Man! Come down
> from the cross, and we will believe thee.
> Aha, thou who wouldst build the temple in three
> days,
> Thou hast nails in thy hands now . . .
> Thou hast wood . . . go on and build thy temple."

> "If thou be the Christ . . . prove it to us . . . Come on
> down from the cross!"

They shouted until they were hoarse.
The noise was so great that only a few of them standing near
the Cross heard what He said when His lips moved in prayer:

"Father, forgive them, for they know not
what they do."

One of the thieves, drugged and half-drunk, cried out to Jesus:

"Can't you see how we suffer?
If you are the Son of God, take us down from these
crosses. Save us and yourself."

The thief cried for salvation—but only for salvation from nails
and a cross—not for salvation from himself and the hell that
his own deeds had wrought.
Then pain gripped him, and he began to curse and to swear,
blaming Jesus for the pain.

But the other turned his head so that he could see Jesus,
and he said to his companion:

"Dost thou not fear God, seeing thou art in the same
condemnation? And we indeed justly, for we have
broken their laws . . . but this Man hath done
nothing amiss."

Then he said to Jesus, "Remember me when Thou comest
into Thy kingdom."
And Jesus, His face drawn with suffering, but His voice
still kind, answered:

"This very day when this pain is over, we shall be
together . . . Thou and I . . . in Paradise."

And the man, comforted, set his lips to endure to the end.

The sun rose higher and higher.
Time oozed out slowly like the blood that dripped from
the cross . . .
Jesus opened His eyes again and saw His mother standing
there with John beside her.
He called out the name of John, who came closer.
Strength was fast ebbing away; an economy of words
was necessary . . .

"Thou wilt take care of her, John?" . . .

And John, choked with tears, put his arm round the
shoulders of Mary.

Jesus said to His mother: "He will be thy son."
His lips were parched, and He spoke with difficulty.
He moved His head uneasily against the hard wood of the
Cross, as a sick man moves his head on a hot pillow.

The women beneath the cross stood praying for Jesus and
for the thieves.
The centurion was silent, although every now and then he
would look up at Jesus with a strange look on his face . . .
puzzled . . . wondering . . . marveling . . .

The rest of the soldiers had been playing knucklebones in the
shadow of the crosses.
Agreeing that they did not want to tear Christ's tunic—or
seamless robe—they had tossed for it.
The Man on the Cross would not need it again . . .

Then, in the awful words of Matthew:

"And sitting down, they watched Him there."

There before their eyes was being enacted the tremendous drama of the redemption of mankind . . .
And they only sat and watched.

They were unwitting actors in the supreme event of which
the prophets had dreamed . . .
They were witnesses, standing at the crossroads of history.
And they saw—*nothing!*

The sky was growing strangely dark.
A thunderstorm seemed to be blowing up from the mountains
and clouds hid the sun.
Women on the converging highways beyond the Hill took
children by the hand and began hurrying back to the city.
People looked up at the sky and became frightened.
The darkening sun at noon caused bird songs to freeze in fear
as their melodies trailed off in the gathering shadows.
It was an uncanny darkness.

The shouting died away.
Now even the soldiers were silent.
They put away their dice. Their gambling was done.
 They had won . . . and lost.

Suddenly, Jesus opened His eyes and gave a loud cry.
The gladness in His voice startled all who heard it.
For it sounded like a shout of victory:
 "It is finished! Father, into Thy hands
 I commit my spirit."

And with that cry He died.
It was the ninth hour . . .

*   *   *

Yes, "He saved others; himself he cannot save."
But they were wrong as well as right.
Could He not have saved Himself?

He might have followed the advice of His friends and avoided
Jerusalem altogether at the feast time.
He might have left the garden that night instead of quietly
waiting there for Judas.
He might have compromised with the priests—and made a
bargain of future silence with Caiaphas.
Had not Pilate almost pleaded with Him for an excuse,
any excuse, for not sending Him to His death?

He might have made His kingdom political
instead of spiritual.
    That would have pleased and silenced Judas.
He might have chosen the expedient.
As He Himself reminded Peter, He might have called upon
twelve legions of angels to rescue Him and to show His
great power.

Yes, He might have saved Himself.
He had the power; many ways of escape were available . . .
    But then He would never have been our Saviour!

Had not Christ said, "I am the Good Shepherd, the Good
Shepherd giveth his life for his sheep."
Giveth his *life?* . . .

But could not our salvation have been consummated without that final price?
No, for when men sin to the uttermost, when sin sinks to its final degradation, no mere palliatives nor mild remedies can deal with it.

What then?
In a world where death by crucifixion was still possible no polite and perfumed half-measures could suffice.
A blood transfusion was necessary . . .
             rich red blood
             human blood.
And if talk of blood offends us, let us remember that crucifixion would offend us too.

Perhaps we need to be reminded that our religion is not all sweetness and light.
Christianity is much more than pretty pictures of Jesus among flowers and singing birds, moving with a smile among simple folk.
The Gospel is much more than the Golden Rule . . .
    much more than the Christmas story
        and the fair green hills of Galilee.

Christianity deals with reality,
    with life as you and I experience it.
For it recognizes that this is not always a pretty world.
It is a world in which dreadful things can happen.

The faith which is nourished and sustained by the Spirit of God faces frankly these human situations which often make our faith difficult.

More than that, Christianity has a cross at the very heart of it. Leave out Calvary, and Christianity dwindles to a weak and empty cult—to a system of impossible ethics.

It would not be good news to preach that there was no sin in Jesus Christ
    therefore we ought to be like Him.
It is not good news to say that He did no wrong,
    therefore we too ought to be perfect.
It is not good news to say that He left us an example that we should follow . . .
These things are true—but they are not a Gospel.
Christ did not come into the world merely to proclaim
a new morality
    or a code of ethics
        or to set up a new social order.
He did not show men how to work out their own salvation
by good deeds
    by charities
        or by trying to live respectable lives.

He came, He said, "to save that which was lost . . ."
He came to save all those who were lost in the sense that they had lost their way . . .

"How think ye? If a man have a hundred sheep, and
one of them be gone astray, doth he not leave the
ninety and nine, and goeth into the mountains, and
seeketh that which is gone astray?"

Never was there in Him condemnation for the lost . . . only
the desire to help the lost one back to the path . . .
    back to right relations with His Father . . .
        back home again.

Yet He well knew our human willfulness.
He knew that after making allowances for heredity
and environment
            for education
        and example
    and the tyranny of habit,
there is still a central shrine of freedom in every life.

There is a place were *we* do it—and no one else,
    where *we* are responsible for our own choices—
and we know it.

            "All we like sheep have gone astray,
                we have turned every one to his own way . . ."

How would He deal with the iniquity
of our human willfulness? . . .

            "And the Lord has laid on him the iniquity of us all."

"Therefore I will divide him a portion with the great,
   and He shall divide the spoil with the strong;
   because he poured out his soul to death,
   and was numbered with the transgressors;
   yet he bore the sin of many, and made intercession
   for the transgressors."

Then there were the sick . . .
"They that be whole need not a physician," He had said,
"but they that are sick"—
   the sin-sick, the sick of mind, the sick of body.
And He who could not tolerate sickness or disease
   in whom there was a passion for health and wholeness
must somehow deal with that too.

How should He do it? . . .

      ". . . upon Him was the chastisement that
         made us whole,
         and with his stripes we are healed. . . ."

And the last enemy Death . . .
   that final fear lurking deep in every human heart . . .
That enemy too must be put down.

How should He do it?
Who but God could deal with all the sin of the ages . . .
         all the suffering of the flesh . . .
      all the sorrow of the heart?

None but God!

But not a God sitting on a gilded throne high up in
the heavens,

    not some ethereal nebulous God floating about in space
    like a benevolent cloud . . .
    not some four- or five-dimensional Deity created by a
    Greek philosopher . . .
But a God walking through your front door and mine . . .
A God who lives and feels and understands . . .
A God who can sympathize . . . who has explored the vast
treasuries of pain . . .

A God who knows what it feels like to weep . . .
A God who can remember the feeling of a tear trickling down
the cheek . . .

Someone utterly pure—in whom there is no spot
                            nor blemish
                      nor taint . . .
Someone willing to give Himself at whatever cost of pain and
suffering and death within this time process, and in the form
of the life that you and I know . . . taking shape—the body of
a man . . . the form of a servant . . .
    with a voice to speak to us . . .
        a heart to feel for us . . .
            eyes to weep with us . . .
                hands to bless and to be nailed to a cross.

        "Surely he has borne our griefs
            and carried our sorrows; . . .

He was oppressed, and he was afflicted,
> yet he opened not his mouth;
like a lamb that is led to the slaughter,
and like a sheep that before its shearers
> is dumb,
so he opened not his mouth.
By oppression and judgment he was taken away;
and as for his generation, who considered that
he was cut off out of the land of the living,
stricken for the transgression of my people?"

The Gospel message is simply that—that such a thing has come to pass . . .

This is the Good News the church has to proclaim . . .
that there is available for us today a Sin Doctor who will come to you and to me and heal us, if we will but let Him into our lives . . .
Whose gracious spirit will mysteriously steal into our hearts and show us the doorway to a new life . . .

Thus the Gospel is not something to do—
> but something done.
The Gospel is not a demand—
> but a supply.
Not something you can do—
> but something that has been done for you.

And it happened at a certain point in time . . .
> on the brow of a hill shaped like a skull.
It was done for me—and for you—simply because He loves us.

96

Had not Jesus said to His apostles that last memorable night with them in the Upper Room . . .

> "Greater love hath no man than this, that a man
> lay down his life for his friends . . ."

That is why a hideous cross has become the world's symbol of blessing.

*   *   *

It was plain to be seen that the Nazarene was dead.
He had died after only six hours of suffering.
Long enough surely . . .
Yet the Roman centurion who watched could not believe that any crucified one could die in just six hours.
To make sure, one of the soldiers had pierced Christ's side with a spear, and the last remaining drops of His blood were poured out.

Yes, He was dead . . .
There was no need to break His legs in an effort
to hasten the end.

During those last hours, John had tried over and over to persuade Mary to leave—but she would not.
Her son was hanging there . . .

So long as there was a breath of life—no—she would
not leave Him.

But Mary herself was nearing a state of collapse.
When it was over, she flung herself on John's breast . . .

                                  sobbing . . . quietly.
Then John lifted her up, put his arms around her shoulders,
and gently led her down the hill towards home.
And Salome, John's own mother, who had been watching afar
off with some of the other women from the outskirts of the
crowd, seeing the little tableau, left the others and came
running to help.

"That one didn't take long," the soldiers said, as they
prepared to fall in line and march back to their barracks.

"Dead so soon?" inquired Pilate, when Joseph of Arimathea
—a member of the Great Jewish Council—came to him to ask
for the body of Jesus.
According to Roman custom the body of an executed criminal
belonged to the relatives or friends, so that by his request
Joseph had now openly avowed his faith in the prophet.

This request surprised Pilate, for the Councilor was a rich
man and a distinguished one—not the usual type to
acknowledge himself as a follower of the Nazarene.
Not until the centurion, having been summoned, confirmed
the statement that the Galilean was really dead, did Pilate
grant Joseph his request.

    98

In some haste—lest anyone else should meddle in the
matter—Joseph, with Nicodemus to help him, then took down
the disfigured body from the cross.
Gently they wound it in strips of clean linen eight feet long
with spices between the layers—as was the custom
of the Jews.

And as their hands busied themselves with the sad work,
words from the Prophet Isaiah came winging their way into
Joseph's mind.
He had learned them as a child in the synagogue . . .
had often recited them to the elders.
How strange that he should remember them at this moment . . .
    as if they had a special significance . . .
       as if—as if—they were meant for him . . .

        ". . . And they made his grave with the wicked
            and with a rich man in his death,
          although he had done no violence,
            and there was no deceit in his mouth. . . ."

And Nicodemus was remembering too, remembering that
night when he had laid aside his work for the Sanhedrin,
turned down the lamp, and gone out under the stars to ask
questions of the Galilean . . .

"For all the rest of my life," he thought, "whenever the
wind moans or tugs at my robes—I shall be remembering
that musical voice:

" 'The wind bloweth where it listeth, and thou
hearest the sound thereof, but canst not tell
whence it cometh, and whither it goeth: so is
every one that is born of the Spirit . . .' "

And now He was dead . . .
Nicodemus was tortured by the knowledge of all the things
he might have said while Jesus lived.
So many things he might have done . . .

"Now," he thought, "it is too late."
And as he looked at the still face of his Friend, unashamedly
he watched his tears making little smudges on the white linen.

Then Joseph and Nicodemus carried the body of their Lord
to a newly made tomb in the Councilor's garden—a tomb
which he had had hewn out of the rock for himself.

After the Sabbath they would arrange for a burial with
proper ceremony.
All they could do at the moment was to make sure of a decent
provisional burial without interference on the part of
the priests.
It would be enough to roll a great round stone to the door
of the sepulchre, for the evening star was already shining . . .
and no more work could be done until the Sabbath was over.

The two men—and the women, Mary Magdalene, and Mary,
the mother of Joses, who had followed at a distance to see
where the body of their Master was being laid—went away
very silent . . . very sad . . .

100

On the morrow the Roman governor was told that a group
of priests and Pharisees sought audience with him.
Pilate undoubtedly suspected that even yet he was not finished
with the matter of the Nazarene—and he was right.

The priests remembered only too well Pilate's mood when they
had asked that the inscription for Christ's cross be changed . . .
So they selected the most soft-spoken and diplomatic member
of the group and thrust him forward as their spokesman:

> "Sire, we remember that Jesus, that deceiver, said
> while he was yet alive, 'After three days I will
> rise again.'

> "Command therefore, we pray you, that the sepulchre
> be made sure until the third day, lest his disciples
> come by night, and steal him away, and say unto the
> people, He is risen from the dead: so the last error
> shall be worse than the first."

The priests irritated Pilate.
He thought of having washed his hand in the golden bowl
such a few hours before . . . "I am innocent of the blood of
this just person: see ye to it . . ."
But somehow he had not been able to wash his hands of it.
The case kept coming back and back . . .

He leaned forward in his gilded chair and wearily passed his
hands across his eyes.
Then he almost roared at the priests:

101

"No! I will not send a Roman guard. That's nonsense
. . . The man is dead. What care I what his disciples
say? You have your own watch. Make it as sure
as you can . . . Now—go your way—"

And he waved his arm for the priests to be escorted from the
audience chamber.

So—in the ironic words of Matthew:

> ". . . they went, and made the sepulchre sure,
> sealing the stone, and setting a watch."

*　　*　　*

It was still dark . . .
Through the deserted streets of Jerusalem three men were
hurrying, almost running towards the residence of the
High Priest.
In the courtyard a slave lifted a torch to see their faces . . .
"See Caiaphas now? At this hour? Impossible . . .
You will have to wait until the dawn at least."

An hour and a half later the three men reported to Caiaphas
that the tomb of the executed Nazarene—which they had been
set to guard—was empty.
Caiaphas was at first puzzled, then angry, then thoughtful . . .
for the men had no explanation.
Repeated questioning could not shake their story . . .

102

No—they had not gone to sleep . . .
There had been a strange stirring in the garden . . .
They had thought they had heard something . . .
Investigation had found the tomb empty—
That was all—

Caiaphas requested that the men tell their weird story again
later on that day to the elders meeting in plenary session . . .

> "And when they were assembled with the elders,
> and had taken counsel, they gave large money unto
> the soldiers, saying, Say ye, his disciples came by
> night, and stole him away while we slept.

> "And if this come to the governor's ears, we will
> persuade him, and secure you.

> "So they took the money, and did as they
> were taught. . . ."

*   *   *

Meanwhile the despair and disillusionment in Simon Peter's
heart were complete . . .
    despair over the shamefulness of his own denial . . .
        disillusionment over the fate of Jesus of Nazareth.
For Peter and the other apostles had hoped that this One
would redeem Israel.
Now all hope was gone: Christ was *dead* . . .
    hailed as King on the Sabbath before . . .
        dead like a common thief on Friday.

103

"I go fishing," Peter said to the others.
What else was there to do?
Life had to go on, be picked up where they had dropped it
when, at the imperious call of a Stranger, they had
abandoned their fishing nets and left everything to
follow Him. ·

Perhaps away from Jerusalem with its bitter memories, they
could forget.
Perhaps with the sea wind once again fanning their cheeks . . .
      with the rough nets sliding through their fingers . . .
    with the feel of the tug of fish
they could forget a certain Face
   a Voice with music in it
      a Smile . . .
         Perhaps . . .

The women too who had ministered to the little band of
apostles were just as despairing—only, as women will, they
were trying to work out their grief in a different way.

They had watched from a distance as Joseph of Arimathea
and Nicodemus had hastily anointed the body of Jesus.
At the first possible moment they would complete
the anointing . . .
So before light dawned on the Sabbath morning Mary Magdalene, Salome, the mother of James the Greater and of John,
and Mary were on their way to the tomb where Jesus' body
had been laid.

104

As they walked in the half-light, they were preoccupied with one problem . . .

> "And they said among themselves, who shall
> roll us away the stone from the door of
> the sepulchre?"

But even as they pondered . . .

> ". . . when they looked, they saw that the stone
> was rolled away: for it was very great. . . .
>
> "And they went out quickly, and fled
> from the sepulchre; for they trembled and
> were amazed. . . ."

What did it mean?
Someone had tampered with Jesus' tomb.
Perhaps His body had been stolen . . .

But the women were so frightened that they did not wait to investigate.
They had only fled . . .
Mary Magdalene, being younger than the others, outran them.
But ere she had reached the road, she met Simon Peter and John—Simon had planned to pay his last respects before he left for Galilee.
Breathlessly Mary blurted out:

> "They have taken away the Lord out of the
> sepulchre, and we know not where they have
> laid Him. . . ."

The two men were shocked; they too started running, but John outran Peter.
And when they stooped down and saw what was in the sepulchre, they believed.
Believed *what?*
Not, as Mary thought, that Jesus' body had been stolen—
But that Jesus of Nazareth was alive!

John and Peter, as they went into the grave in the garden that first Easter morning, did not know *what* to think—until they saw what was inside the grave—
> *And then they believed.*

The inside of the tomb revealed something that proved the Resurrection.
What was it?
Let us turn to the narrative again and read carefully:

> "Then cometh Simon Peter following him, and went into the sepulchre, and seeth the linen clothes lie. And the napkin, that was about his head, not lying with the linen clothes, but wrapped together in a place by itself. Then went in also that other disciple, which came first to the sepulchre, and he saw, and believed."

In this connection, it is well for us to remember that the stone was rolled away from the door, not to permit Christ to come out, but to enable the disciples to go in.

Notice what it was they saw.
They saw the linen clothes lying, not unwound and carefully folded, as some people appear to think—
   not thrown aside as is a covering when one rises from bed, but lying there on the stone slab in the shape of the body.

True, the napkin had been removed and folded, but the grave-clothes were lying there, mute but eloquent evidence that a living organism had come out.

The grave-clothes lay like the shriveled, cracked shell of a cocoon, left behind when the moth has emerged and hoisted her bright sails in the sunshine . . .
Or, more accurately, like a glove from which the hand has been removed, the fingers of which still retain the shape of the hand.

In that manner, the grave-clothes were lying, collapsed a little, slightly deflated—because there was between the rolls of bandages a considerable weight of spices, but there lay the linen cloth that had been wound round the body of Christ.

It was when they saw *that,* that the disciples believed.

The Greek word here for "see"—*theōrei*—is not to behold as one looks at a spectacle, not to see as the watch-maker who peers through his magnifying glass.
It means to see with inner light that leads one to conclusion.

It is perception
    reflection
        understanding—more than sight.
Do you *see?*

It is to see, as one who reasons from the effect to the cause.
And when John and Peter reasoned from what they saw
in the tomb, they arrived at the conclusion
        the unshakable
    unassailable
  certain conviction
that Jesus Christ had risen from the dead.

*   *   *

But Mary Magdalene, still weeping, lingered at the edge
of the garden.
Along with the other women, she had come to find a dead body
. . . and had been shocked to find the grave empty.

She thought it had been broken open—grave-robbers perhaps.
She did not know . . .
She could not think clearly.
Only one thought seems to have absorbed her soul—
    the body of the Lord had been lost . . . she must find Him!

108

She ran as never before back towards the empty tomb, with the speed and unawareness of time and distance that grief or fear or love can impart . . .

> "But Mary stood without at the sepulchre weeping;
> and as she wept, she stooped down, and looked into
> the sepulchre . . . and she turned herself back, and
> saw Jesus standing, and knew not that it was Jesus.
>
> "Jesus saith unto her: 'Woman, why weepest thou?
> Whom seekest thou?' "

And John tells us that she thought He was the gardener. She fell at His feet, her eyes brimming with tears—her head down—sobbing, "Sir, if thou hast taken Him hence, tell me where thou hast laid Him, and I will take Him away."

To her tortured mind there was a gleam of hope that perhaps the gardener, for some reason known only to him, had moved the body . . .
She was red-eyed . . .
She had not slept since Friday . . .
There had been no taste for food . . .
She had been living on grief and bereaved love . . .

> "Jesus saith unto her . . . 'Mary . . .' "

His voice startled her . . .
She would have recognized it anywhere.

She lifted her head with a jerk . . . blinked back the tears from her eyes and looked—right into His eyes.

She knew . . . her heart told her first and then her mind . . . She saw the livid marks of the nails in His hands and looking up into His face, she whispered:

"Rabboni!"

The loveliest music of that first Easter dawn is the sound
of those words echoing in the Garden . . .
    His gentle . . . "Mary . . ."
        and her breathless . . . "Master!"

Mary had come prepared to weep—
    Now she could worship.
She had come expecting to see Him lying in the tomb—
    She had found Him walking in the newness of
    resurrected life.

                    *   *   *

So much had happened in those last few days.
To Cleopas and his friend, the week that had closed seemed
like a terrible dream.

Event had followed event in a swiftness which had left no
time for meditation.
As the two men walked along the winding road to Emmaus,
it was of these things they spoke.

There had been Christ's entry in triumph into the Holy City.
To all of them, it had seemed that—at last—their Messiah
would enter into His own.
Surely, the days of Roman occupation would now soon be over.
Exactly when the Messiah would announce Himself and
declare their independence, they did not know.

Joyously, the multitudes thronged around Him,
awaiting the good news.

Then, swiftly, there had been woven around the Nazarene
a net of intrigue—soon to be drawn tighter and tighter.

There had been that night when Judas had turned on his heel
and left the Upper Room to keep his treacherous rendezvous.
There had been Jesus' strange words of dismissal, as He had
watched Judas disappear into the night.

Then the scene that followed in the garden
out on the hillside . . .
Would they ever forget it?
In the silence of the night, Jesus prostrate in prayer . . .
       the bright Syrian stars seeming to fill the sky . . .
     the gnarled olive trees casting grotesque shadows . . .
   a swinging lantern coming up the winding path . . .
the rabble of temple doorkeepers and temple police, who
had laid aside their brooms and their keys long enough
to come out with Judas to arrest the Galilean . . .
How could they ever forget?

As Cleopas and his companion talked, they became
more and more engrossed.
Their words came pouring out in a torrent of recollection.

There had been the despicable kiss of Judas . . .
   the arrest itself . . .

the foolhardiness of Peter with his little sword . . .
   the return to the city . . .
      Peter's blasphemous denial by the fire . . .
    the all-night vigil.

The rest was an agony of painful memories . . .
   the scourging of Christ in front of Pilate's palace . . .
    the blood-thirsty cries of the mob . . .
     the march to Golgotha . . .
      those awful moments,
  when the sound of a hammer had echoed across the valley.

There had been the ravings and curses of the thieves
on their crosses . . .
   the strange eerie darkness . . . and the earthquake . . .
And the death of Him whom they had learned to love, of Him
whom they had called . . . "Master."

So engrossed were the two men in these memories, that they
did not notice the approach of a Stranger.
Suddenly, there He was walking beside them.

And He said to them. "What is this conversation which you
are holding with each other as you walk?"

And they stood still, looking sad.
Then one of them, Cleopas, answered him,
   "Are you the only visitor to Jerusalem who does not know
   the things that have happened there in these days?"

115

And He said to them, "What things?"

And they said to Him, "Concerning Jesus of Nazareth, who
was a prophet mighty in deed and word before God and all the
people, and how our chief priests and rulers delivered Him up
to be condemned to death and crucified Him.
But we had hoped that He was the one to redeem Israel.
Yes, and besides all this, it is now the third day
since this happened.

"Moreover, some women of our company amazed us.
They were at the tomb early in the morning and did not find
His body; and they came back saying . . . He was alive . . ."

And He said to them, "O foolish men, and slow of heart
to believe all that the prophets have spoken!
Was it not necessary that the Christ should suffer these things
and enter into His glory?"

And he began with Moses and all the prophets and explained
to them all the Scriptures that referred to Himself.

Thus did the walk of seven and a half miles pass quickly.
And when they reached Emmaus, the sun was fast sinking
behind the copper hills.

The shadows were long . . . soon it would be dark.

The two men begged the mysterious Stranger to spend the night with them, or at least to share their evening meal. Still they did not know who He was.

Why?

Largely because Christ was the last person these disciples expected to see.

Had they not seen Him die?

Had they not watched His head fall limp on His shoulders?

It had seemed so absurd to them as they had stood at the foot of the Cross and remembered His words:

> "Whosoever believed in me, though he were dead, yet shall he live . . . and whosoever liveth and believeth in me shall never die . . . ."

Then to see Him die—right there before their eyes . . .

They had not been able to grasp the glorious truth that life hereafter is not dependent upon the physical at all . . . is not material but spiritual.

So the disciples imagined that Jesus of Nazareth could not possibly be alive unless He were just as He was before . . .
   dependent upon the same material limitations that bounded their lives.

And so they sat down at last to eat their evening meal.

The Stranger stayed with them and, in the most natural way in the world, gave thanks before He took bread in His hands.

There was something in the way He gave thanks . . .
　　as He took bread . . .
　　　　reached across the table . . .
　　　　　　broke the bread with a characteristic gesture . . .
　　　　　　　and the folds of His robe fell back . . .
Perhaps they saw the livid red marks of the nails in His hand.
But whatever it was, in that instant they knew . . .
They knew!
And He was gone.

It wasn't possible!
It couldn't be . . .
But they had seen Him with their own eyes.
Then the women were right!
And they rose and ran—ran, not walked,
all the seven and a half miles back to Jerusalem to tell the
other disciples the incredible news.

But they found some of the disciples completely unwilling
to believe what they were reporting.
Salome and Mary, the mother of James the Less and of Joses,
had been there much earlier in the day and had already told
them the news of the empty tomb.
Then Mary Magdalene had appeared—her eyes shining
like stars—saying . . .
　　　　"I have seen the Lord!"

But these women were emotional creatures.
How could their testimony be accepted as credible?

> "And their words seemed to them as idle tales,
>   and they believed them not."

Then Peter and John had appeared not only talking about the
empty tomb, but offering an explanation for it—
an explanation they could not, would not accept.
Resurrection? Impossible!
How could intelligent men believe *that?*

And now the breathless Cleopas and his friend with the same
words that Mary Magdalene had used . . .

> "We have seen the Lord!"

Seen a dead man? Impossible!
Had everyone suddenly gone crazy?

Thomas, one of the disciples, thrust out his jaw and
stepped forward.
He said what some of the others had been wanting to say . . .

> "I don't believe you . . . What we've all been through
>   must have temporarily unhinged your minds . . .
>   I would have to see the Lord for myself. Not only
>   that, except I shall see in his hands the print of the
>   nails, and put my finger into the print of the nails,
>   and thrust my hand into His side,
>   *I will not believe.*"

It was eight days before Thomas got his proof.

Once again the disciples were gathered together,
Thomas among them.
Suddenly Jesus was with them in the room.
He singled Thomas out, smiled at him:

> "Reach hither thy finger, and behold my hands;
> and reach hither thy hand, and thrust it into
> my side; and be not faithless, but believing."

Thomas was all but overwhelmed.
Gone was all his blustering skepticism
He fell to his knees . . . All he could say was . . .

> "My Lord and my God."

Simon Peter witnessed this.
There was now no doubt in his heart . . .
Something tremendous had indeed happened.
The Christ who had been crucified was alive . . .
Life could never be the same again!

Yet something else troubled Simon, ate at him.
He was still nursing deep and bitter shame, still smarting with
the scaring iron that had eaten into his very soul.

He had denied his Lord.
How could he ever face Him again?

Whenever Simon was deeply troubled, always he went back
to his nets.
"I go a-fishing," he would say . . . and this time six of his
friends decided to go with him.

120

There came the night when the men had worked hard and
had caught nothing.
As they rowed back towards shore, discouraged and
in comparative silence, they saw Someone standing
on the beach in the early light of morning.
The sea was calm—calm as a millpond—and a light
early-morning mist still clung to the surface of the water.

"Children, have ye any meat?"

And when they replied in the negative, the voice called:

"Cast the net on the right side of the ship,
and ye shall find."

They had nothing to lose in following the Stranger's advice.
Over the side went the nets again, this time with success—
so much success that the nets were in danger of breaking.

They were now getting closer to the shore, and the mist was
beginning to lift.
They could see flames leaping from a fire on the beach, and
this mysterious Figure waiting for them to beach their boat.

"It is the Lord," said John, and that was enough for Simon.
Here was the opportunity for which he had longed—to tell
the Lord that he loved Him—to show how well he knew Him.
Without a moment's hesitation, he jumped overboard and
waded ashore.

And then comes the loveliest record of God dealing with a
penitent sinner . . .
Its tenderness and understanding come stealing into our own
hearts like the perfume of crushed flowers.

As they sat round the fire, cooking some of the fish they
had caught and baking their loaves of bread on the live coals,
Jesus suddenly turned to Simon . . .

"Simon, son of Jonas, lovest thou me
more than these?"

Simon was a little puzzled at the question:

"Yes, Lord, Thou knowest that I love Thee."

Christ looked him straight in the eyes . . .

"Then—feed my lambs."

Then again He asked:

"Simon, son of Jonas, lovest thou me?"

Simon was a little hurt. Why would the Lord *keep* asking?

"Yes, Lord, Thou knowest that I love Thee."

"Then—feed my sheep."

But when the question came the third time, light began to
dawn for Simon.
For every one of Simon's earlier denials Jesus was now asking
a pledge of love.
This was His way of making everything all right again.

When next we see Simon, he is Simon no more—
but Peter—the Rock.

We see him fearless and eloquent
fire in his eyes
and his voice vibrant with conviction,
melodious with good news.

His own will has gone; his Master's will has taken its place. Peter stands up and preaches the Gospel of his crucified and risen Lord.

Furthermore he is preaching it in Jerusalem, at the storm-center of the enemies of the Nazarene.

Implicit in the whole situation is the fact that on the day of the Crucifixion the disciples did not ever expect to see Christ again.
The Resurrection was the last thing they expected.
Their belief in it was not some fantastic idea, wafted in from the swamps of fevered imaginations.
It was not some romantic wish out of their dream-house, not the result of wishful thinking.
For it had come as a complete shock,
    unexpected
        bewildering.

There is no more adamant fact in the records than the changes that came over these men.
Jerusalem had been anything but impressed with the way Christ's disciples had conducted themselves during the arrest and trial of the Nazarene.
His followers had certainly not been courageous.
In fact, they had all either fled to save their own lives or followed at a great distance.

Peter was so fearful that he had even denied having known the Nazarene.

Then after their Master's death, the band of disciples had stayed in hiding with the doors locked—"for fear of the Jews."

Yet after that first Easter morning, we find these same men
    timid
        frightened
           ineffective
preaching openly, with no fear of anyone.

Their personal conviction rings like a bell through the pages of the New Testament . . . steady and strong . . .

> "That which we have heard with our own ears,
> seen with our own eyes, handled with
> our own hands, declare we unto you."

And of what were they so sure?
That Jesus Christ was alive—but no spiritual resurrection this—not just the perpetuation of a dead man's ideas.

No, by a Resurrection they meant that on a certain Sabbath, suddenly, at a given time between sunset and dawn,
in that new tomb which had belonged to Joseph of Arimathea,
there had been a fluttering of unseen forces . . .
    a rustling as of the breath of God moving through the garden.

128

Strong immeasurable life had been breathed back into the
dead body they had laid upon the cold stone slab;
And the dead man had risen up
        had come out of the grave-clothes
      had walked to the threshold of the tomb,
    had stood swaying for a moment on His wounded feet,
and had walked out into the dewy garden alive for evermore.

It was so real to them that they could have almost heard
the whispered sigh as the spirit had fluttered back into the
worn body . . .
Almost catch a whiff of the strange scents that had drifted
back to Him from the tomb
    of linen and bandages . . .
        of spices—myrrh and aloes . . .
            and close air and blood.

Furthermore, they were saying these things in the same city
that had sought to destroy the Christ,
    right at the door of the stronghold of the priests,
        a thousand paces from the tomb where Christ
        had been laid.

Christ's enemies would have given anything to have refuted
their claims.
One thing would have done it—so simply.
If only they could have produced a body.
But they could not . . .

So they tried everything else they could think of to silence
these fishermen, tax collectors, farmers, carpenters,
shepherds, housewives . . .
>imprisonment
>>threats
>>>scourgings
>>>>stonings and death.
Nothing succeeded in silencing them.

There would come the time when Peter would actually stand
before Caiaphas and the Sanhedrin, as Jesus had done, and
nothing but flaming words of courage would pass his lips:
>>"Whether it be right in the sight of God to hearken
>>unto you more than unto God, judge ye.
>>For we cannot but speak the things which we have
>>seen and heard. . . ."

Now it takes a very great conviction to change men
so drastically.
Nor do men persist in a lie or even a delusion, if every time
they insist on its truth, they are driving nails
into their own coffins.

Men do not invent a story, so that they can be crucified
upside down, as Peter eventually was . . .
>or have their head chopped off, like Paul, outside the
>city of Rome,
>>or be stoned to death—like Stephen.

130

A self-hypnotic illusion may sustain men for a time—
but not for long.
In the long run, an illusion does not build character strong
enough to stand great hardship, great persecution.
Only the bedrock truth can do that!

Moreover, men who are merely fooling themselves do not
become purposeful men
    well-integrated men with self-sustaining qualities
    of leadership . . .
as these erstwhile timid apostles became.

And here is something else—it was their continuing
fellowship with their Risen Lord through the years which
became the integrating
    guiding
       sustaining
power of their lives.

Through His spirit they had guidance and strength . . .
They had His wisdom
    His peace
       and His joy.
They had boldness and courage and they had power . . .
    qualities that they had not had until after the first
    Easter morning.

They now felt that they still were in touch with Him . . .
    in a different way—yes—but in a more powerful way.
They knew that He was still with them, even
as He had promised . . .

"Go ye into the world and lo, I am with you always."

They felt that! They knew it!
The promises He had made to them before His death were now fulfilled, and they (men like Cleopas and his friend) went up and down in the land . . .
They crossed the sea.
They shook the Roman Empire until it tottered and fell.
They changed the world.

This is the fact we in this Twentieth Century cannot ignore.

Through the nineteen centuries which have followed in every land there have been men and women who have experienced the same fellowship . . .
   who have felt the same power in their lives . . .
      who have had the same peace and inner serenity . . .
         who have had the same joy and the
         same radiant victory.

They were not crackpots, morons, nor lunatics.
Included among them were some of the greatest minds the world has ever seen . . .
Some of the most brilliant thinkers
                  philosophers
               scientists
            and scholars . . .
They were not frustrated personalities who fled the world of reality and found refuge in the dug-outs of their own wistful escapes from life.

132

On the contrary, most of them have been radiant souls filled with an abiding joy, living to the full every golden hour, and tasting the deepest joys of life.

Dismiss, as you will, the sentimentality, the hysteria and the wishful thinking that may be born in times of crisis and danger, there is still a residue of hard, stubborn testimony from men who met Him during the Second World War . . .

For example, while they drifted on life-rafts on the ocean . . . who came home through dangerous skies "on a wing and a prayer" . . . who met Him in the dog-watch of many a long night in dangerous waters.

And you, too, may have that fellowship with the Risen Christ. Indeed you will not believe the fact of the Resurrection for yourself until the living Christ lives in your own heart.
When you have in your own life that sense of His nearness and His power—ah, then, you too will *know!*

Your life today may be guided by Christ . . .
Your problems may be solved by His wisdom . . .
Your weakness may be turned into strength by His help . . .
Your struggles may become victories by His grace . . .
Your sorrows may be turned into joy by His comfort.

To you there may come the same wonderful changes that have come to other men and women all down through the years.

This is the reality that can be yours—this comradeship with the Resurrected Christ through His spirit is available now . . .

   To the man in the street . . .

      to the government clerk . . .

         to the anxious mother . . .

            to the confused school boy or girl.

This is the real meaning of Easter.
Forget the bunny rabbit and the colored eggs.
Forget the symbols of spring that so often confuse and conceal the real meaning of what we celebrate on that day.

No tabloid will ever print the startling news that the mummified body of Jesus of Nazareth has been discovered in old Jerusalem.
Christians have no carefully embalmed body enclosed in a glass case to worship.
Thank God, we have an empty tomb.

The glorious fact that the empty tomb proclaims to us is that life for us does not stop when death comes.
Death is not a wall, but a door.
And eternal life which may be ours now, by faith in Christ, is not interrupted when the soul leaves the body,
for we live on . . . and on.

There is no death to those who have entered into fellowship with Him who emerged from the tomb.
Because the Resurrection is true, it is the most significant thing in our world today.
Bringing the Resurrected Christ into our lives, individual and national, is the only hope we have for making a better world.
"Because I live, ye shall live also."

That is the message of Easter.

JESUS

GUIDEPOSTS ASSOCIATES, INC., Carmel, N.Y.

LOVED

THEM

by Sam Patrick and Omar Garrison

CONTENTS

MARY THE MOTHER

"And in the sixth month the angel Gabriel was sent from God unto a city of Galilee, named Nazareth, to a virgin espoused to a man whose name was Joseph, of the house of David; and the virgin's name was Mary."

—Luke I:26,27

MARY, the mother of Jesus, was referred to by the Jews as the daughter of Eli; but early Christian writers called her the daughter of Joakim and Anna.

She was related by marriage to Elizabeth, the wife of Zacharias, the priest.

The fact that she was already with child when she was married to Joseph made her an object of much ridicule by her contemporaries, who did not believe in her accounts of a visitation from Gabriel, nor of the annunciation that she was to become the virgin mother of the Messiah.

The story connected with the birth of Jesus, the flight into Egypt, and the presentation of her Son at the Temple are all related in full in the Gospels.

Mary's profound thoughtfulness and maternal love are indicated in the New Testament, which says that "his mother kept all these things in her heart."

Perhaps no mother in history suffered the long travail for her son, as Mary in her deep concern for Jesus, from the night of His birth in Bethlehem to the final tragic night of Golgotha.

Scripture mentions her only four times following the reappearance of Jesus and the beginnings of His ministry after 18 years of absence or silence.

The first is the marriage at Cana in Galilee, at which she was present with her Son. The second was at Jerusalem at the last Passover, observed by Jesus. The third was at the foot of the Cross, when Jesus committed her to the care of John, His beloved disciple with the words, "Woman, behold thy son," and to John, "Behold thy Mother."

Finally, in the days following the Ascension, Mary met with the faithful disciples in the upper room, where they "all continued with one accord in prayer and supplication."

JOSEPH

". . . the angel of the Lord appeared unto him in a dream, saying, Joseph, thou son of David, fear not to take unto thee Mary thy wife: for that which is conceived in her is of the Holy Ghost."

—Matthew I:20

LITTLE OF JOSEPH's personal history is told in the New Testament. He is described as a "just man," who resided in Nazareth. He was of the house and the lineage of David.

We know him as a quiet man, who understood and believed the message of the angel who warned him of danger to the Infant Jesus, and kept him constantly alert to the snares woven in the minds of the Child's enemies.

He comes to us in the role of the protective father, the tireless watcher over his Charge, the careful provider of His early physical needs.

Scriptural history of Joseph ends with the account of the Holy Family's journey to Jerusalem for the Passover, when Jesus was 12 years of age.

But it is evident by implication that he died before the trial and crucifixion, since Jesus upon the Cross gave the care of His mother into the keeping of the beloved disciple.

There is an apocryphal story told of Joseph and his carpenter's shop, where he is said to have taught Jesus his trade.

He was showing the young Boy how to carve wood with the grain. Jesus watched closely and then duplicated the operation with understanding and skill.

"You can always know a wood by its grain," Joseph told Him. "And knowing the grain, you can mould it to the form you wish.

"It is like the nature of man. Know this, and you can anticipate his thoughts, and direct these as you wish, if you have a reason that is good."

Jesus understood this parable, the story goes. He told Joseph:

"I am aware of the Time ahead. And I will meet it."

3

JOHN THE BAPTIST

"There was a man sent from God, whose name was John."

—*John I:6*

TALL, SOLITARY, HOMELESS—wrapped in a camel's skin, his hair depending upon his shoulders, his eyes burning with the zeal of evangelism—such was John the Baptist.

Born when both his parents were of advanced age, he went into the wilderness when still very young, to meditate and to purify himself after the manner of the yogis of India. He soon attracted a multitude "from every quarter."

Jesus, then nearing His 30th year, journeyed from Galilee to the Jordan, where the "wild man," the Baptizer, immersed the penitent in the waters of the river for a symbolical cleansing, even as he told them of the coming Messiah, who would baptize with fire.

When John saw Jesus approaching, he said: "Behold the Lamb of God, which taketh away the sin of the world."

Jesus, about to embark upon the three brilliant last years of His earthly life, marked the Change with baptism in the Jordan.

John the Baptist understood this. He knew that his prophecy was about to be fulfilled.

A crowd gathered upon the banks as Jesus entered the river, to witness His baptism. It was the last day of harvest, and their spirits were high. To their superficial view, the baptism of Jesus was like that of other "sinners" who had come to have their spiritual stains washed away. But such was not the case with John.

"And straightway coming up out of the water, he saw the heavens opened, and the Spirit, like a dove descending upon him. And there came a voice from heaven, saying, Thou art my beloved son, in whom I am well pleased."

The mission of John the Baptist was fulfilled. The final mission of Jesus had begun.

PETER

"And when Jesus beheld him, he said, Thou art Simon the son of Jona: thou shalt be called Cephas, which is by interpretation, A stone."

—John I:42

B EFORE MEETING JESUS, this disciple was known as Simon ("hearer"). He was the son of a successful fisherman named Jona.

His brother Andrew, a follower of John the Baptist, had been present when the evangelist had baptized Jesus, and when he had said, "Behold the Lamb of God, that taketh away the sin of the world."

Andrew hurried to tell Simon of the event. "We have found the Messiah," he declared excitedly, and took Simon to see Jesus.

Jesus, immediately upon seeing him, recognized him, and gave him the surname by which he was ever afterward to be known—Peter, the rock.

But before the Resurrection and Ascension, when he set out to establish the Church in the world, there is little doubt that Peter still thought of the Messiah as the political figure foretold by the Jewish prophets.

In the apostle's evangelical history, his character is portrayed with great clarity.

Yet there were contradictions in his make-up, as there are in that of all men. Complete renunciation of the world was not easy for him. When Jesus said, "It is easier for a camel to pass through the eye of a needle than for a rich man to enter into the kingdom of God," Peter was a little dismayed.

Peter's challenge was, in fact, the challenge that has faced all men in all ages, including our own. He had the same weaknesses, and some of the same strength. In overweening self-confidence, he cried: "Lord, I am ready to go with Thee both into prison and to death," then denied that he knew the Man.

But in his strength he defied the Roman emperors, and according to tradition, was crucified head downward by Nero in Rome.

7

ANDREW

"One of the two which heard John speak, and followed him, was Andrew, Simon Peter's brother."

—John I:40

ANDREW, like his brother Simon Peter, was a fisherman residing in the town of Bethsaida on the shore of Galilee.

A follower of John the Baptist, by whom he was directed to Jesus, he at once recognized the Nazarene as the Messiah, and hastened to conduct Simon to Him.

In the Gospel lists of the Twelve, he is always named among the first four who were called to discipleship.

The Scriptural narrative indicates that during Jesus' ministry, Andrew was a constant companion. He was present at the Last Supper; he was among the group of disciples to whom Jesus appeared after His resurrection; he witnessed the Ascension; and he shared in the glories of Pentecost.

Although he, like almost all the others of the Twelve, did not show open revolt during the trial and crucifixion of his Master, Andrew apparently did not lack courage.

Ancient writers say that he went as a missionary through Sythia and adjoining countries, an undertaking which, in those days involved not only the usual hazards of travel, but the likelihood of arousing the wrath of pagan rulers who mercilessly put to death the preachers of the new doctrine of Christianity.

Andrew's travels are said to have taken him through Thrace, Macedonia, Cappadocia, Galatia, Bithynia and Achaia. It is conjectured that he founded a church in Constantinople, but there is no conclusive historical record of his having done so.

Most historians agree that his career had its tragic end at Patrae, a city of Achaia. There the proconsul, Aegeas, outraged by Andrew's preaching, ordered him to offer a sacrifice to the pagan gods. The Apostle refused, whereupon the Roman governor had him scourged and crucified.

JAMES SON OF ZEBEDEE

"And when he had gone a little farther thence, he saw James the son of Zebedee, and John his brother, who also were in the ship mending their nets."

—Mark I:19

*J*AMES, like his younger brother John, was a well-to-do fisherman on the Lake of Galilee.

At the Master's call, both left their nets to become "fishers of men."

Jesus called the brothers Boanerges, meaning "Sons of Thunder," apparently because of their dynamic, burning faith.

This impetuous zeal which characterized both brothers is evident in the passage (Luke IX:51-56) which tells of the Samaritans' refusal to receive Jesus because He was enroute to Jerusalem, the capital city of their enemies, the Jews.

"And when his disciples James and John saw this they said, Lord wilt thou that we command fire to come down from heaven, and consume them even as Elias did?"

But Jesus curbed their spirit of retaliation. He told them:

"The Son of man is not come to destroy men's lives, but to save them."

Instead of creating a public tumult, as well as further resistance to His message, Jesus went to another village.

James, along with John the Beloved, went with Jesus to the garden of Gethsemane on the night of agony before the Crucifixion. He was also a witness to the Transfiguration and, later, to the Ascension.

According to Scripture (Acts XII:1,2), James was arrested on orders from King Herod Agrippa shortly before Passover in the year 44, and was beheaded.

Secular history tells us that the accuser of James, who had brought him before the judges who condemned him was so deeply impressed by the apostle's faith and constancy, even under torture, that the informer was himself converted to Christianity, and suffered the same fate as James.

The characteristic of James that makes him an immortal prototype of the true believer was his steadfast faith in Jesus and His mission.

JOHN THE APOSTLE

"When Jesus therefore saw his mother, and the disciple standing by, whom he loved, he saith unto his mother, Woman, behold thy son!"

—John XIX:26

W HATEVER DISTINCTIONS or com-
mendable attributes the other apostles may have had, it was John whom Jesus
loved with the intimate, understanding affection of brother, companion, and
trustworthy friend.

At the Last Supper, John was seated not only next to Jesus, but leaned his
head upon the Master's breast. And in the agonized hour of His death, looking
down upon the little group of faithful who had followed Him even to the Cross,
Jesus commits His mother to the care of John.

Again, it was the beloved disciple who first recognized the resurrected
Jesus on the Sea of Galilee, when He appeared in the morning twilight on the
dim shore.

John was a son of Zebedee, an apparently well-to-do fisherman of Bethsaida. Jesus nicknamed him and James, his brother, Boanerges, meaning "Sons of
Thunder." Such a designation should serve to dispel the impression that might be
given of John by early Christian art, which often depicts him as of a passive,
meek, almost epicene nature.

In the face of extreme persecution by a group headed by Saul of Tarsus,
John resolutely stood his ground. The Scripture tells of his presence in Jerusalem
15 years after Saul's (later Paul) first visit to that city.

John's later history is not recounted in the New Testament. But according
to tradition, he left Jerusalem and went to Ephesus. It is said that during the
reign of Domitian, he was arrested and taken to Rome, and later sent into exile
on the Isle of Patmos.

It was while there, apocryphal accounts say, that he was given the visions
of the last days, part of which he wrote down in his Book of the Revelation.

It is conjectured that he lived to an extreme old age, the dates of his death
having been set variously from A.D. 89 to A.D. 120.

13

PHILIP

"Now Philip was of Beth-saida, the city of Andrew and Peter."

—*John 1:44*

THE BIBLE tells very little about this Apostle, save that he was a fellow townsman of Andrew and Peter; and apparently among the first of that little band of Galileans to follow Jesus from the outset of His ministry.

It is clear that Philip had a practical, perhaps even a mathematical turn of mind, for when the hungry multitude that followed Jesus had to be fed, He turned to Philip and asked:

"Whence shall we buy bread, that these may eat?"

Philip apparently made a quick estimate of the number of persons in the crowd and told Jesus:

"Two hundred pennyworth of bread is not sufficient for them, that every one of them may take a little."

Like others of the disciples, Philip often found it difficult to understand Jesus' words, and His profound meanings.

Jesus told the little company: "If ye had known me, ye should have known my Father also; and from henceforth ye know Him, and have seen Him."

But this assurance only confused Philip. He said, "Lord, shew us the Father, and it sufficeth us."

A little sadly perhaps, Jesus asked Philip then:

"Have I been so long time with you, and yet hast thou not known me, Philip? He that hath seen me hath seen the Father; and how sayest thou then, Shew us the Father?"

Philip was with the other disciples at Jerusalem after the Ascension. And again on the day of Pentecost he is mentioned.

But following that day, according to tradition he went as a missionary to Phrygia and was later martyred and buried at Hierapolis.

15

BARTHOLOMEW

"And when it was day, he called unto him his disciples: and of them he chose twelve, whom also he named apostles; Simon, (whom he also named Peter,) and Andrew his brother, James and John, Philip and Bartholomew . . ."

—Luke VI:13,14

BARTHOLOMEW WAS ONE of the Apostles whose life story has been lost to us during the centuries that have passed since he was first called by Jesus to be one of the Twelve.

A number of authorities believe he is the same person as Nathanael, mentioned in the Gospel of John (I:45-51).

This opinion is based on the fact that Bartholomew is not a proper name, but merely served to identify him as the son of Tolmai.

Moreover, the name Bartholomew is never mentioned in the Gospel according to John. But in the latter Evangelist's list of Apostles, Nathanael is the name given in the place accorded to Bartholomew in the other three Gospels.

Scholars reason, therefore, that John may have referred to him by his given name, where the other three Gospel writers followed the Hebrew custom of calling him the son of Tolmai.

It was Philip who first told Nathanael of Jesus. And, John relates, Nathanael replied somewhat contemptuously, "Can there any good thing come out of Nazareth?"

But upon first seeing Jesus, Nathanael followed Him as readily as the other disciples, declaring, "Rabbi, thou art the Son of God."

According to traditions of the early Church, Bartholomew became a missionary to the East, preaching in Mesopotamia, Persia, Egypt, and Armenia.

Legends say he was martyred in Albanopolis, Armenia. The manner of his death is variously reported as having been crucifixion, beheading, and being flayed alive.

The immortal Michaelangelo apparently inclined to the latter story, for in his famous painting, "The Last Judgment," a flayed Bartholomew is shown holding his own skin in his hand.

THOMAS

"Except I shall see in his hands the print of the nails, and put my finger into the print of the nails, and thrust my hand into his side, I will not believe."

—John XX:25

T HOMAS, called Didymus, which signi-
fies a twin, has come to be known as the embodiment of man's doubt.

Although he readily became one of the disciples of Jesus, he was never fully aware of the Master's real identity and power.

Countless times Thomas had witnessed Jesus' answers to all the questions put Him by a curious multitude. He had witnessed the miracles, and had heard Jesus say, "Said I not unto thee, that, if thou wouldest believe, thou shouldest see the glory of God."

But believing came hard to Thomas. The doubting apostle evidently regarded Jesus as a man with unusual powers of suggestion, by which He controlled the minds of others, and consequently their bodies.

He remained quietly observant during the days of his association with Jesus. Secretly, he was convinced that a logical, reasoning mind would require more proof than a Carpenter would be able to provide that He and God were one, and that He spoke the truth.

To Thomas, Truth was what could be known, not something deeply intuited or inwardly sensed and experienced.

He was not satisfied even with the testimony of his eyes and his ears. He had to add the proof of his hands as well.

All the while that Jesus talked of His Kingdom to come, a Kingdom "not of this world," Thomas dreamed of a tangible, substantial, political realm on earth.

When his friends brought him the joyful news that Jesus had indeed risen from the dead as He said He would, Thomas refused to believe it until he had felt the Savior's wounds.

Said Jesus: "Blessed are they that have not seen, and yet have believed."

19

MATTHEW

"And as Jesus passed forth from thence, he saw a man, named Matthew, sitting at the receipt of custom: and he saith unto him, Follow me . . ."

—Matthew IX:9

M

ATTHEW, originally called Levi, was a native of Galilee, but Scripture does not say of which city, nor of which tribe of Israel.

Although a Jew, he apparently enjoyed the confidence of the Romans, whom he served as a publican or tax collector. His job was that of collecting custom duties and fees from persons and commodities that passed over the Sea of Galilee, or along the portion of the Damascus road that skirted it.

After Jesus called him to be an apostle, Matthew, who was evidently a man of means, gave a feast at his home. In addition to Jesus, who was probably guest of honor, he invited others of the disciples, several publicans, and friends.

His idea in giving such a banquet would appear to be twofold: to mark the end of one way of life and the beginning of a new way as a disciple of Jesus; and to give his former companions an opportunity to know something of the new Gospel that had changed his life.

Matthew's personal stature grows when seen in the perspective of his personal life and environment prior to his meeting Jesus: a man of education and wealth, the handler of money—that symbol of materialism and worldly greed—he had only to be bidden, "Follow me," and he turned his back resolutely and finally upon the past.

After the Ascension, Matthew remained in Jerusalem with the other Apostles. On the day of Pentecost he received the gift of the Holy Spirit.

Christians are greatly indebted to Matthew for his version of the Gospel, in which he carefully preserved the words and parables of Jesus.

The Bible does not tell how long Matthew remained in Judea after the Ascension, but a fifth-century church historian relates that he was martyred in Ethiopia, where he had gone as a Christian missionary.

JUDE

"And Judas the brother of James . . .

—Luke VI:16

JUDE, who was known also as Judas Thaddeus and Lebbeus, was another son of Alpheus and, consequently, a close relative of Jesus.

Beyond being mentioned in the catalogue of Apostles, the New Testament tells us very little about Jude, except indirectly. For example, as one of "the brethren of the Lord," Jude may have been married. It is also said that he did not fully believe in Jesus and His mission until after the Resurrection.

The only incident related by Scripture concerning Jude during the ministry of Jesus occurs in John XIV:22-23, but it gives some insight into the character of the Apostle.

Jude asks Jesus: "Lord, how is it that thou wilt manifest thyself unto us, and not unto the world?"

Jesus replied: "If a man love me, he will keep my words: and my Father will love him, and we will come unto him, and make our abode with him."

Jude is author of one of the General Epistles which bears his name. During the third and fourth centuries, several of the churches raised doubts as to its canonicity, but it was later considered canonical by all.

In his epistle (or letter), Jude warns the congregation against a number of false teachers and heresies of that time, and exhorts the Christians to persevere in the faith. Hastings, in his "Great Texts of the Bible," says:

"He sounds the final note of warning. The key word is 'kept.' Those who embrace the faith are preserved unto the day of presentation; those who reject and oppose the faith are 'reserved' unto the day of retribution."

Little is known of Jude's history following Pentecost. Some ancient sources say he traveled and preached in Arabia, Syria, Mesopotamia, and Persia.

SIMON THE ZEALOT

". . . and Simon called Zelotes."

—Luke VI:15

A SIDE FROM THIS BRIEF REFERENCE (and similar references in the other Gospels), the New Testament tells us very little of Simon, except that he was called by Jesus to be one of the twelve disciples.

Luke indicates that he was a member of the Zealots, a Jewish sect which adhered strictly to Mosaic ritual, and advocated the assertion of religious liberty by force of arms.

Elsewhere he is called the Canaanite, referring not to the place of his birth, but to the Hebrew word signifying "to be zealous." Luke, who wrote his Gospel in Greek, merely used the Greek term meaning the same thing.

The sect of Zealots is believed to have been organized by a fierce patriot known as Judas the Galilean who, when Judea was made a Roman province, publicly urged the people to resist Roman rule, and to refuse to pay taxes.

The Jewish historian, Josephus, paints a very derogatory picture of the Zealots in their later history during the siege of Jerusalem under Vespasian.

It may well be that Simon the Zealot was one of the followers of Jesus who believed that He might be a political deliverer who would overthrow the hated rule of Rome.

In one of his most widely quoted poems, the American poet, Ezra Pound, tried to imagine the thoughts of Simon the Zealot, following the Crucifixion. The work is called, "Ballad of the Goodly Fere," and one of the stanzas quotes the disciple as saying:

"A master of men was the Goodly Fere
A mate of the wind and sea.
If they think they ha' slain our Goodly Fere
They are fools eternally."

JUDAS ISCARIOT

"He spake of Judas Iscariot the son of Simon: for he it was that should betray him, being one of the twelve."

—*John VI:71*

OF ALL THE TWELVE who were called to be disciples, the character of Judas remains the most mysterious.

The Gospel writers tell us nothing of his life or background before he met Jesus, and very little of his association with the Master, except always to identify him as the betrayer.

But, as Dr. Hales observes, "the treachery of Judas Iscariot, his remorse and suicide are occurrences altogether so strange and extraordinary that the motives by which he was actuated require to be developed as far as may be done, where the Evangelists are in a great measure silent concerning them."

It is obvious that Judas had some overwhelming weakness, some ruling passion that made him, when under its influence, powerless to resist evil.

But what was that weakness? Was it covetousness, as the Gospel narratives imply—a lust for money that was so great that he stole even from the disciples themselves?

If that were true, why was Judas made steward and almoner for the group, receiving contributions and overseeing their redistribution?

An interesting apocryphal source states that Judas Iscariot's weakness was wine. While this account has no Scriptural support, it is a more rational explanation of his behavior. For, even in our own day, alcoholics and drug addicts often sacrifice everything, even those they love, on the altar of their inveterate habit.

The Gospels tell us that, stricken with remorse, Judas tried to undo the betrayal of Jesus, and returned the 30 pieces of silver, which the priests refused, and which were eventually used to buy a potter's field.

In profound despair, Judas went out and hanged himself; but in the act, apparently the rope broke and he fell down a steep precipice at Aceldama where "he burst asunder in the midst." (Acts I:18).

JAMES SON OF ALPHAEUS

"And he ordained twelve, that they should be with him . . . Andrew, and Philip, and Bartholomew, and Matthew, and Thomas, and James the son of Alphaeus . . ."

—Mark III:14,18

No NAME in the New Testament has caused quite so much confusion as that of James.

The reason is that in different places we read variously of James the son of Alphaeus, James the brother of the Lord; and of James the Less.

Are all these one and the same person? Catholic scholars for the most part say yes. Many Protestant authorities agree with them.

But then another question arises. What is meant by the designation, "brother of the Lord"?

Catholic interpreters assert that the Greek word, "adelphos," used in this reference, can mean step-brother or even a near relative.

Therefore, they argue, James was not the brother of Jesus in the literal sense—that is, he was not the son of Mary, the Virgin. It is more likely, they contend, that he was the son of the Virgin's sister, and therefore a cousin of Jesus.

In the early Church, the Greek fathers believed him to be the son of Joseph by a first marriage. Latin writers of the same period, however, all regarded James as the cousin of Jesus, since they taught that Mary remained a virgin all her life.

It is said that after the martyrdom of St. Stephen, the other Apostles chose James to preside over affairs of the Church in Jerusalem. Hence, he is sometimes referred to as the Bishop of Jerusalem.

According to the historian Hegesippus, who lived toward the end of the second century, James made a public declaration of his faith from one of the Temple ramparts, and was hurled to the ground by angry scribes and Pharisees. He was not killed by the fall, so his attackers then stoned him. As he was being killed, so the account goes, he called upon God to forgive his murderers.

MARY MAGDALENE

"And certain women, which had been healed of evil spirits and infirmities, Mary called Magdalene, out of whom went seven devils . . . and many others, which ministered unto him of their substance."

—*Luke VIII:2,3*

"WOMEN LOVED JESUS," says Papini in his incomparable "Life of Christ." "They would have liked to be His sisters, His servants, His slaves; to serve Him, to set bread before Him, to pour Him wine, to wash His garments, to annoint His tired feet and His flowing hair."

Next to His mother, the woman who was nearest to Jesus, who followed Him fearlessly to the very foot of the cross, and to whom He appeared first when He rose from the dead, was Mary Magdalene.

She was so called because she came from the town of Magdala, in Galilee, where she lived during the early part of her life.

Scripture does not include many details of her life before she met Jesus, but most Biblical scholars agree that she was a woman of considerable means and position in her society.

Although popular opinion has long made her a kind of arch-type for the "repentant sinner" and fallen woman, there is not a shred of evidence to support such a view.

On the contrary, it is more likely that she was, as one ancient writer says, an educated woman, daughter of a wealthy Greek ship owner, who taught Platonic philosophy.

In any event, from the moment she met Jesus, until His final reappearance from the tomb, she was His devoted and intimate follower.

She accompanied Him and ministered to Him on His last journey from Galilee to Jerusalem, and, together with Mary, His mother, and John, the Beloved Disciple, wept for Him on Calvary.

After the Crucifixion, she helped prepare His body for entombment.

LAZARUS

". . . he cried with a loud voice, Lazarus, come forth. And he that was dead came forth, bound hand and foot with grave clothes . . ."

—John XI:43,44

IT IS EASY to understand the confusion, unbelief, and astonishment of the people who witnessed this event.

Lazarus, the friend of Jesus and the brother of Martha and Mary, had been dead four days. The practical Martha told Jesus, when He asked them to take away the stone from before the dead man's tomb:

"Lord, by this time he stinketh."

Saddened a little by the lack of faith, even in His closest friends, Jesus ignored the objections and lifted His face heavenward in a brief prayer:

"Father, I thank thee that thou heardest me. And I knew that thou hearest me always: but because of the multitude that standeth around I said it, that they may believe that thou didst send me."

Then He called into the dark tomb, "Lazarus, come forth."

Lazarus came stumbling out, still wrapped in his grave clothes.

"Loose him," said Jesus, "and let him go."

No doubt, as Lazarus walked again as a man and flexed his muscles painfully as feeling returned to his limbs, he tried to recall what it had been like to be dead and entombed.

It is quite likely that he could recall only a blank state of unconsciousness, similar to sleep, for Jesus had said:

"Our friend Lazarus sleepeth; but I go that I may awake him out of sleep."

Both Martha and Mary reproached Jesus with the same words before He had recalled Lazarus from the tomb:

"Lord, if thou hadst been here, my brother had not died."

The answer He gave Martha is the answer that lives as the solace of all Christians who mourn for their loved ones:

"I am the resurrection and the life: he that believeth on me, though he die, yet shall he live; and whosoever liveth and believeth on me, shall never die."

MOTHER OF JOHN

"And many women were there beholding afar off, which followed Jesus from Galilee, ministering unto him: Among which was . . . the mother of Zebedee's children."

—*Matthew XXVII:55-56*

B IBLE SCHOLARS agree that the name of the Beloved Disciple's mother was probably Salome.

They base this belief on the fact that the passage in Mark XV:40, parallel to that quoted above, refers to her by that name.

It is further conjectured on reliable grounds that she was probably the sister of Mary, the mother of Jesus.

From the scanty account given of her in the Gospel narrative, it is evident that she, like her sons John and James, was a devoted follower of Jesus, who was present at the Crucifixion and assisted at His entombment.

Matthew, in his Gospel (XX:20) relates that on one occasion she came to Jesus with her two sons, "desiring a certain thing of him."

"And he said unto her, What wilt thou? She saith unto him, Grant that these my two sons may sit, the one on thy right hand, and the other on the left, in thy kingdom."

But Jesus told her:

"Ye know not what ye ask. Are ye able to drink of the cup that I shall drink of, and to be baptized with the baptism that I am baptized with?"

Both John and James, says Matthew, assured Jesus that they were able to drink of His bitter cup. And Jesus agreed that "ye shall drink indeed of my cup, and be baptized with the baptism that I am baptized with: but to sit on my right hand and on my left, is not mine to give, but it shall be given to them for whom it is prepared of my Father."

A CHILD BLESSED

"Then were brought unto him little children, that he should put his hands on them, and pray: and the disciples rebuked them."

—*Matthew XIX:13*

J ESUS LOVED little children because in the purity of their hearts and the innocence of their enchanted world, they often understood Him better than did His gruff, mature disciples.

So He never turned them away, whether their mothers had brought them to be blessed, or to be cured of some illness.

There is a beautiful story, unsupported by Scripture, told of how Jesus one day comforted a child whose dog had died. Listen:

This story was told by John, who has been named the Beloved Disciple, unto peoples of the North countries:

John said: "I remember once He found a small boy weeping for his dog that lay dead beside him. And Jesus lifted up the child and told him:

"'Animals live a different way from men and they see what few men see on earth. And often he befriendeth man, as thy furry friend lingereth now to draw thy vision from the earth that ye may see beyond this world in which men also die.'

"Jesus lifted the small hand and placed within its palm a token—a small shell that He had found on the shore that morning, and had carried in His tunic. He explained that the small creature who had once lived within this house had left it.

"'Now pause a moment, watch the shell and listen,' He told the child. And the child gave rapt attention to the little shell, and listened to the story of the sea, learning how a small shell *could* house a living creature who might depart, and yet not die. And that it is God's plan that everything in the experience of boys and men must change."

BLIND BARTIMAEUS

". . . And as he went out of Jericho with his disciples and a great number of people, blind Bartimaeus, the son of Timaeus, sat by the highway side begging."

—*Mark X:46*

A s it is to this day in the Holy Land, blindness was a common affliction in the time of Jesus.

It is easy to imagine the unpleasant appearance of Bartimaeus, the blind beggar of Jericho—the sightless, staring eyes, encrusted with dried secretion and infested with flies.

Probably the disciples turned away from him in disgust. But Jesus perceived the strong light of faith that shone through his inner darkness, and led him, through his feelings, to know that he was in the presence of the Master.

It is evident that Bartimaeus did so recognize Jesus, for he addressed Him by his Messianic title:

"Jesus, thou Son of David, have mercy on me."

Mark tells in his gospel that "many charged him that he should hold his peace." But blind Bartimaeus, groping towards the Radiance that suddenly shone in the heaven of his personal night, would not be suppressed. He cried out louder than ever.

"And Jesus stood still, and commanded him to be called. And they called the blind man, saying unto him, Be of good comfort, rise; he calleth thee.

"And he, casting away his garment, rose, and came to Jesus.

"And Jesus answered and said unto him, What wilt thou that I should do unto thee? The blind man said unto him, Lord, that I might receive my sight.

"And Jesus said unto him, Go thy way; thy faith hath made thee whole. And immediately he received his sight, and followed Jesus in the way."

In our day, it is by such faith as that of this blind beggar of Jericho that we receive our spiritual sight, and can follow Him "in the way."

THE OBSESSED BOY

"There came to him a certain man, kneeling down to him, and saying, Lord, have mercy on my son: for he is lunatick, and sore vexed . . ."

—*Matthew XVII:14-15*

B ECAUSE SCRIPTURE refers to this unfortunate boy as a "lunatick," some modern writers have asserted that the child was merely afflicted with epilepsy.

They argue that in Greek usage the term (meaning to be moonstruck) was commonly applied to that disease.

However, the New Testament account is unequivocal in stating that the boy was possessed by an unclean spirit:

"He rebuked the foul spirit, saying unto him, Thou dumb and deaf spirit, I charge thee, come out of him and enter no more into him.

"And the spirit cried and rent him sore, and came out of him: and he was as one dead; insomuch that many said, He is dead."

The child's father had previously brought the boy to Jesus' disciples to be healed, but they were unable to cure him. "I spake to thy disciples that they should cast him out; and they could not."

From the description of the boy's symptoms, related by the father, we know that he was not only given to seizures in which he foamed at the mouth, but that he was deaf and dumb. During his attacks, he often endangered his own life by falling into the fire or into the river or lake.

Mark, in his Gospel, points out that it was the father's faith which made it possible for his son to be healed.

"Jesus said unto him, If thou canst believe, all things are possible to him that believeth."

And in response to Jesus, the boy's father cried out, with tears in his eyes:

"Lord, I believe; help thou my unbelief."

The result of this father's humble, but powerful faith, was the expulsion of the evil that controlled his son.

OBSESSED BOY'S FATHER

"And when they were come to the multitude, there came to him a certain man, kneeling down to him, and saying, Lord, have mercy on my son . . ."

—*Matthew XVII:14-15*

WHY DID THIS FATHER bring his son to Jesus to be healed after the Galilean's own disciples had tried and failed?

Perhaps even he could not have answered that question.

Somewhere deep within him was a faith he did not recognize himself. For true belief is knowledge without knowing the source. Thus, on the one hand he could say, "I believe," and on the other, "Help thou my unbelief."

His faith had deep root in his consciousness. So he knew Jesus could heal his son, because this knowledge was an impression placed in his mind by his soul.

His belief, then, was the touchstone by which the gifts of life and healing were his for the asking.

How can such a belief be recognized?

It can be known by the trust placed in Him to fulfill His promise: "If ye shall ask anything in my name, I will do it." And to ask in His name is to find release from all other ideas concerning that which one has believed before.

So the grieving father looked upon Jesus that day and learned that his first and greatest need was not simply that his son should be cured, but that he should believe.

This struggle in the father's heart, between recognition and trust and an involuntary human will to disbelieve is the struggle of all men.

And victory is often possible only through the severest trial—in this case a father's anxiety about his only child.

Even the disciples, those closest to Jesus, had not fully resolved this conflict. Luke tells us that when they witnessed the miracle, "they were all amazed at the mighty power of God."

SIMON OF CYRENE

"And as they came out, they found a man of Cyrene, Simon by name: him they compelled to bear his cross."

—*Matthew XXVII:32*

THE SADDEST and most terrible procession in recorded history is approaching Jerusalem's Gate of Gardens.

Led by a mounted Roman centurion and a small company of soldiers, and followed by a mixed crowd of jeering, curious, and sympathetic spectators, three men drag heavy crosses toward the Hill of Skulls where they are to be crucified.

Two of them are convicted thieves. The third is Jesus of Nazareth, whose crime was that He set love above the law of the Temple, and sought to bring into the dark and unbelieving thoughts of men the light of their Creator.

Weak from the night-long ordeal of interrogation, floggings, and inhuman torture, this Man of Sorrows staggers under the weight of the heavy rood. At last, able to go no farther, He falls to the ground, and lies utterly exhausted beneath His massive burden.

The Centurion turns in his saddle and looks down at the Man stretched beneath the cross. He realizes at once that it is a physical impossibility for Jesus to bear the cross another step.

In the crowd, the Centurion's eye falls upon Simon, a Greek Jew from Cyrene, on the north coast of Africa.

"You!" commands the Centurion. "Take up this man's cross and follow us."

The Cyrenian has no choice but to obey. And the Scripture does not tell whether he performed his task willingly and with pity for the innocent Man who had fallen; or whether sullenly and with resentment for both Jesus and the hated Roman authorities.

But for Christians over the past two millenia, Simon of Cyrene is the most envied man in the New Testament story. Because in that important moment, he was chosen to bear upon his husky shoulders a small part of God's burden.

45

CAIAPHAS

*"Now Caiaphas was he, which gave counsel to the Jews, that it was expedient
that one man should die for the people."*

—*John XVIII:14*

THIS ANSWER, which the high priest, Caiaphas gave Nicodemus, when the latter sought to defend Jesus, was the keynote of the prosecution throughout.

"What do we? for this man doeth many miracles. If we let him thus alone, all men will believe on him: and the Romans shall come and take away both our place and nation."

The personal animosity, the greed, the hypocrisy which hid behind this noble motive is apparent only when we study the character and activities of Caiaphas.

In the first place, most of the money changers and merchants Jesus had driven out of the temple had operated their bazaars not only with the high priest's suffrance, but were in fact owned by the sons of Annas, the father-in-law of Caiaphas.

Caiaphas was of the sect of Sadducees, who denied that any moral law was of divine authority, save that which had been written. Moreover, they rejected the belief of resurrection after death, and of reward or punishment once a man had died.

When Jesus was brought before Caiaphas, the high priest judged Him according to the written law.

"I adjure thee by the living God, that thou tell us whether thou be the Christ, the Son of God?"

And Jesus, who had remained silent up to this point, answered: "Thou hast said; nevertheless I say unto you, hereafter shall ye see the Son of man sitting on the right hand of power, and coming in the clouds of heaven."

Upon hearing this, Caiaphas ripped his clothes (a traditional act), saying: "He hath spoken blasphemy; what further need have we of witnesses?"

47

THE MONEY-CHANGER

"And Jesus went into the temple of God, and cast out all them that sold and bought in the temple, and overthrew the tables of the moneychangers . . ."

—Matthew XXI:12

J

ESUS SAW IN MONEY the symbol of man's greed, sensuality and lust for power over the lives of other men.

He saw the coins, stamped with the image of a cruel temporal ruler, passed from hand to eager hand, bearing a contagion more deadly than the plague.

It is not strange, therefore, that when Jesus saw how the money-changer profaned even the house of God with the corruption of his commerce, He resorted to the only recorded act of violence in his ministry.

The money-changer made a personal profit by exchanging coins current in Jerusalem for those brought by Jews from distant parts of the Roman empire.

According to Hebrew custom, every Jew of twenty years or over had to pay yearly during the month of Adar a half-shekel to the temple treasury in Jerusalem.

The religious law required that this tribute should be paid in Jewish coin. Consequently, the money-changers did a thriving business, exchanging half-shekels for Greek and Roman coins.

For this service he could exact a stated fee, known as a *kolbon*. But, taking advantage of the ignorant and the uninformed, he extracted from the stranger whatever sharp practice would yield.

The doves mentioned by Matthew in this passage, and the sheep and oxen included in John's account, were sold to be used as sacrifices at the temple.

Profit thus extorted by fraud, by trading upon men's religious obligations, Jesus regarded as the worst kind of robbery.

"It is written," he told them, "My house shall be called a house of prayer; but ye have made it a den of thieves."

THE WOULD-BE DISCIPLE

"And another also said, Lord, I will follow thee; but let me first go bid them fare-well, which are at home at my house."

—Luke IX:61

AMONG THOSE who gathered often to listen to Jesus, there were always some who, moved by His words, wanted then and there to become disciples.

This man was one of them. He had not stopped to consider what discipleship really meant: a total change in one's familiar habits and thinking.

Family responsibilities, possessions, home, self-concern—all these had to become secondary for the man who would follow in the way of the Master.

Jesus demonstrated this in His own life from the first. When He was only twelve and His mother, believing Him lost, finally found Him questioning the learned doctors at the Temple, He told His parents:

"How is it that ye sought me? wist ye not that I must be about my Father's business?"

Years later, during His ministry, as He talked to the people, "his mother and his brethren stand without, desiring to speak with him." But His answer was:

"Who is my mother? and who are my brethren?"

Did this mean that earthly relations were of no importance? Not at all. The tenderest and most filial bond existed between the Savior and His mother. Even as He was dying upon the Cross, He thought of her welfare and committed her care to John, the Beloved Disciple.

What He did mean was that God and the service of God must come first.

"He that loveth father or mother more than me is not worthy of me," He had told his own disciples.

But this would-be disciple could not understand this. He had thought that following Jesus could be merely an exciting avocation, like music, art, or philosophy.

51

PONTIUS PILATE

"Pilate therefore went forth again, and saith unto them, Behold, I bring him forth to you, that ye may know that I find no fault in him."

—*John XIX:4*

PONTIUS PILATE, who became procurator of Judea under Tiberius Caesar in A.D. 26, was a product of Roman society during the early Empire.

He was military in bearing, tactless, skeptical, arbitrary. Almost from the first day of his arrival in Judea, there existed an implacable hatred between him and the people he ruled.

Twice before the trial of Jesus, he had been forced to yield to the will of the populace, or risk open rebellion that might cost him his position.

The first time occurred when he brought army standards bearing the likeness of the Roman emperor into Jerusalem, thus profaning the holy city. After five days of uproar and rioting, he removed them.

On another occasion, the Jews forced him to remove a set of Roman votive tablets from Herod's palace, which he occupied in Jerusalem.

Pilate knew that Jesus was innocent. He had secret spies among the people who had reported almost daily on the Nazarene's activities.

Moreover, there is good reason to believe that Pilate's wife, Claudia Procula, had actually met Jesus, and was one of His secret followers.

During the trial, she sent Pilate a message, warning him to "have nothing to do with that just man."

But, "when Pilate saw that he could prevail nothing, but that rather a tumult was made, he took water and washed his hands before the multitude, saying, I am innocent of the blood of this man . . ."

In the most critical decision of his career, the "fearless" Roman had again bowed to the shouting, factious, bloodthirsty mob.

Tradition says he never forgot this tragic hour. A few years afterward, in exile, "wearied with misfortunes," he killed himself.

PILATE'S WIFE

"When he was set down on the judgment seat, his wife sent unto him, saying, Have thou nothing to do with that just man . . ."

—*Matthew XXVII:19*

MATTHEW GIVES us only this brief glimpse into the life of Pilate's wife.

Perhaps her only importance for the writer of the Gospel narrative was that one moment when her life touched that of Jesus and she intervened to save Him because she had "suffered many things this day in a dream because of him."

An apocryphal writer says that her name was Claudia Procula, which suggests that she may have belonged to the noble and influential family of that name in Rome.

The fact that Pilate was able to take her with him to Judea lends support to such a view. There was a Roman law forbidding pro-consuls to take their wives with them when they went to rule in foreign lands.

Her reference to Jesus as "that just man" suggests a previous and accurate knowledge of Him. Had she heard His message, and was she, too, a secret disciple, like Nicodemus?

Such a thing is not impossible. As several historians have pointed out, Roman women of that day were beginning to show a great interest in Eastern faiths, which offered more personal promise and satisfaction than the Latin cults. In Rome itself, a great number of patrician women had been initiated into the Mithraic religion.

Scripture does not tell what Pilate's reaction was to his wife's note. But there is little doubt that it strengthened his own resolve to release Jesus.

The fact that Pilate did not have the personal courage to persist in that resolve, even at the possible cost of his own position, was no fault of his wife.

The Greek Orthodox Church thought so highly of Claudia, in fact, that she is revered as a saint by members of that denomination.

A MAN BORN BLIND

"And as Jesus passed by, he saw a man which was blind from his birth."

—John IX:1

THE EYES THAT were turned toward Jesus that day as He passed through the streets of Jerusalem, were like empty slates upon which the Man of Galilee could write a story of God's love.

Knowing that this man had been blind from birth, the disciples asked Jesus:

"Is his affliction the result of sins committed by him or by his parents?"

This question implies a belief among the followers of Jesus in reincarnation—a Greek concept that was current among many Jews at that time.

But Jesus told His disciples:

"Neither hath this man sinned, nor his parents: but that the works of God should be made manifest in him."

That the blind man had indeed been prepared to play a part in the miracle which followed is evident in the fact that he instantly believed in the power of Jesus and followed His remarkable directions for a cure.

It required great faith to believe that even a Messiah could give sight to one born blind. Medical men of all ages have agreed that total blindness from birth is virtually incurable. That is why the blind man's neighbors, in their own unbelief, said:

"Since the world began was it not heard that any man opened the eyes of one that was born blind."

But this blind beggar who all his life had promised only his prayers in return for alms, was so deeply moved by the unseen Stranger that he was willing to believe even in the impossible.

For, having done his bidding and washed in the pool of Siloam, the man of darkness looked for the first time upon the Light of the World.

DINER AT THE FEAST

"And when one of them that sat at meat with him heard these things, he said unto him, Blessed is he that shall eat bread in the kingdom of God."

—*Luke XIV:15*

J

ESUS HAD ACCEPTED the invitation of a prominent Pharisee to take sabbath dinner in his house. The Savior was aware that He had been asked not because the host wished to honor Him.

Instead, he had hoped to trap Him into some violation of the strict laws governing observance of the sabbath.

But Jesus took the occasion to counter the diners' hostile and argumentative attitudes with a parable warning them that by their hypocrisy and indifference, they would lose their places at the great feast of His Kingdom in the last days.

This unnamed diner provided the point of departure for the parable by repeating the often expressed hope of the Jews at that time:

"Blessed is he that shall eat bread in the kingdom of God."

Answering him in a gentle, but earnest tone, Jesus told of the Great Supper, which John in Revelation called "the marriage supper of the Lamb."

It was God Himself who had sent His servant to announce that the Great Feast of salvation had been prepared and was spread for all who would come.

But those who received the invitation—the religious leaders who regard themselves as the only rightful heirs of God's kingdom—began to find excuses.

So the poor, the maimed and the halt—the multitude held in such contempt by the Pharisees—were bidden to the Feast.

And still room remained for more guests at His Table. So the outcasts from the highways and the hedges—the Gentiles, the unbelievers, and the lowliest of men—were brought to the Supper "that my house may be filled."

A heavy silence fell over the feast, as Jesus concluded:

"I say unto you, That none of those men which were bidden shall taste of my supper."

THE ADULTERESS

"And the scribes and Pharisees brought unto him a woman taken in adultery . . ."

—John VIII:3.

THE TIME is early morning, the place an outer courtyard of the temple.

Jesus sits surrounded by perhaps a score of people. They are the curious, the confused, the hopeful. He looks deep into their eyes as He tells them of the Truth that will make them free.

Suddenly, as He is speaking, there is a commotion outside the entrance. Several scribes and Pharisees—those crafty enemies of Jesus—rudely shove a woman before them into the enclosure.

She holds back, shielding her face with an arm. Her hair and clothes are in sad disarray; she is trembling and frightened.

"Master," they say, "this woman was taken in adultery, in the very act. Moses in the law commanded us that such should be stoned: but what sayest thou?"

They hope He will defy the Mosaic law, so they can accuse Him before the high priest.

But Jesus does not answer them. He stoops down and with His finger traces words upon the dusty earth. If the woman was caught "in the very act," then her partner in sin must be known also. Who is he? Among her accusers?

Angrily, they press Him for an answer. He straightens up.

"He that is without sin among you, let him first cast a stone at her."

There is an embarrassed silence. The accusers' own secret sins return to haunt them like evil spirits. One by one, beginning with the eldest, they slip away, "convicted by their own conscience."

Jesus looks at the woman. He asks her: "Woman, where are those thine accusers? Hath no man condemned thee?"

"No, Lord," she answers, daring to look at Him for the first time.

"Neither do I condemn thee: go and sin no more."

OFFICIAL WHOSE DAUGHTER
WAS HEALED

"... *Behold, there came a certain ruler, and worshipped him, saying, My daughter is even now dead: but come and lay thy hand upon her, and she shall live.*"

—*Matthew IX:18*

L UKE, IN HIS gospel account of this incident, tells us that the ruler's name was Jairus, and that he was governor of one of the synagogues—perhaps at Capernaum.

Moreover, we learn that it was the man's only daughter who was ill and that she was about twelve years of age.

Although the literal phrase in Matthew declares that "my daughter is even now dead," it is clear from Luke's narrative that the official meant that his daughter lay at the point of death when he left home, and probably had died by the time he reached Jesus.

But Jesus reassured the man who had sought Him out, fallen at His feet in humility, and expressed so great a faith ("lay thy hand upon her and she shall live").

"Fear not," He told Jairus, "believe only, and she shall be made whole." By the time they arrived at the house funeral rites were already in progress.

As was the custom, professional mourners were weeping and wailing loudly, accompanied by rude musical instruments. The practice was similar to the traditional Irish wake.

Jesus turned the mourners out of the house, and allowed only Peter, James, and John to go in with Him.

He told the mourners:

"Weep not; she is not dead, but sleepeth."

But, like skeptical materialists of all ages, "they laughed him to scorn, knowing that she was dead."

Jesus took the girl by the hand and called to her, saying: "Maid, arise."

"And her spirit came again, and she arose straightway: and he commanded to give her meat."

WOMAN WHO TOUCHED HIS ROBE

"And, behold, a woman, which was diseased with an issue of blood twelve years, came behind him, and touched the hem of his garment."

—*Matthew IX:20*

JESUS WAS on His way to the house of Jairus to raise that official's daughter from the dead, when this nameless woman in the crowd about Him, demonstrated the power of intense faith.

She said within herself:

If I may but touch his garment, I shall be whole."

She did not realize that Jesus would be aware of her touch, made with such intense hope, based upon implicit faith.

In the multitude that accompanied Him, many must have brushed against Him, or plucked at His sleeve with this or that request.

But the touch of this woman was different. It was the hand of faith, reaching out to salvation.

And Jesus immediately turned and asked those about Him:

"Who touched me?"

Everyone denied having done so. Then Peter said:

"Master, the multitude throng thee and press thee, and sayest thou, Who touched me?"

Jesus explained that somebody had touched Him, "for I perceive that virtue is gone out of me."

When she saw that her act had been discovered, the woman came forward, trembling. Falling at Jesus' feet, she confessed to Him and to everybody present why she had touched Him, and how she had been instantly healed.

Jesus, who was always gentle with the troubled in spirit, said:

"Daughter, be of good comfort. Thy faith hath made thee whole; go in peace."

As Prof. F. Davidson observes, "It is still true that while multitudes throng Jesus, it is the few who touch Him."

ARMY CAPTAIN AT CAPERNAUM

"And when Jesus was entered into Capernaum, there came unto him a centurion . . ."

—*Matthew VIII:5*

U NLIKE MOST soldiers of the Roman legion who occupied Palestine during the time of Jesus, this centurion had a great deal of respect for the Jews and their religion, and was considered by them to be a godly man.

Luke reports that the elders of the Jews spoke to Jesus on his behalf, saying:

"He loveth our nation, and he hath built us a synagogue."

It has been conjectured that, since Galilee was ruled by Herod Antipas, the centurion probably commanded some Roman troops maintained by that tetrarch at Capernaum.

When the Roman sought the favor of Jesus, it was for the healing of a servant "who was dear to him," but was on the point of death—reduced to utter impotence and misery by some form of palsy or paralysis.

The character of the centurion is all the more remarkable when viewed in its proper historical perspective. In those days, a servant was little better than a slave.

When he asked Jesus to help the sick servant, Jesus told the Roman:

"I will come and heal him."

But the centurion had so much faith in the Master's prowess that he said, "Lord, I am not worthy that thou shouldest come under my roof: but speak the word only, and my servant shall be healed."

Just as the soldiers obeyed his commands, the centurion said, so the forces of good would heal the sick servant at the command of Jesus.

When Jesus heard this, He turned to His followers and said:

"Verily I say unto you, I have not found so great faith, no, not in Israel."

And He healed the centurion's servant "in the self-same hour."

THE GREEK WOMAN

"For a certain woman, whose young daughter had an unclean spirit, heard of him, and came and fell at his feet . . ."

—*Mark VII:25*

This woman whose persistent faith was tested by Jesus and found to be based upon true conviction, is referred to by Matthew as "a woman of Canaan," and by Mark as "a Greek, a Syro-phenician by nation."

Even as it does today, adversity—the illness of her child—led her to implore the mercy of God.

Hearing of the Nazarene, she sought Him out and fell at His feet, crying:

"O Lord, thou son of David; my daughter is grievously vexed with a devil."

But Jesus did not immediately reply. Instead, He exercised her faith and her perseverance in belief. His disciples wanted Him to send her away, for they said, "She crieth after us."

It was the first time that a person who was not a worshipper of the God of Israel had asked Jesus for miraculous aid.

"I am not sent but unto the lost sheep of the house of Israel," Jesus said, testing her further.

But this did not shake her belief in Him. Instead, she came and worshipped Him, saying, "Lord, help me."

But still Jesus tested her sincerity and faith. "It is not meet to take the children's bread, and cast it to dogs," he said, using the familiar phrase of the time which referred to nations other than Israel as "dogs."

"Truth, Lord," she replied in her humility, "yet the dogs eat of the crumbs which fall from their masters' table."

Whereupon, Jesus granted her request, at the same time commending her for her intuitive knowledge of God's mercy to all who respond to Him:

"O woman, great is thy faith," He said. "Be it unto thee even as thou wilt."

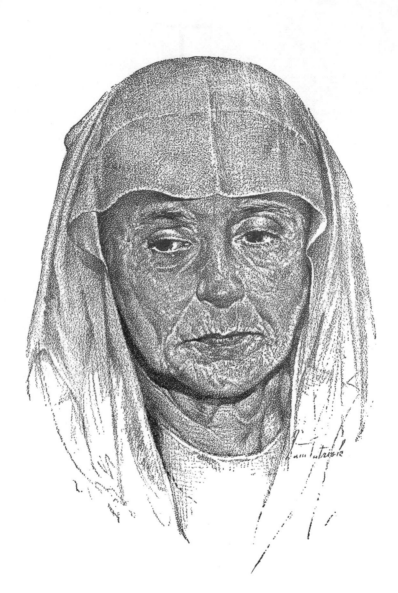

PETER'S MOTHER-IN-LAW

"*. . . And Simon's wife's mother was taken with a great fever; and they besought him for her.*"

—*Luke IV:38*

I was the Sabbath, and Jesus, together with some of the disciples, had just left the synagogue.

Mark tells us that "when they were come out of the synagogue, they entered into the house of Simon and Andrew."

There they found that Simon's mother-in-law was seriously ill with some kind of fever.

"And he stood over her, and rebuked the fever; and it left her: and immediately she arose and ministered unto them."

It is noteworthy that when Jesus healed the sick, the cure was instantaneous and complete. There followed no period of convalescence or recuperation from the ravages of the disease.

Simon's mother-in-law was so wonderfully restored to health that she "arose and ministered unto them."

Like most women of Jesus' time, Simon's mother-in-law exercised an important influence in her home. Not only was she in charge of such domestic matters as supervision of the housekeeping, but also of preparation of meals. Even women of rank or wealth were not exempt from this responsibility.

So it is not unusual that, as soon as she was well again, her first thoughts would be of her guests—especially of the important guest who had just cured her infirmity.

Serving the crowds who always followed Jesus was no small task, as was shown by the miracle of the loaves and fishes.

And, at sunset, as soon as the Sabbath was ended, "all they that had any sick with divers diseases brought them unto him; and he laid his hands on every one of them, and healed them."

71

NICODEMUS

*"Now there was a man of the Pharisees named Nicodemus, a ruler of the Jews:
the same came to Jesus by night . . ."*

—*John III:1,2*

NICODEMUS was the prototype of today's lukewarm believer.

His Soul recognized and acknowledged Jesus, but his mind urged caution. It told him: you are a man of influence and position in your community, but this Man is a vagabond. You are learned in the laws of the synagogue, but this Man speaks of a kingdom beyond the law and beyond life. If you are seen among His followers, will you not be compromised in the eyes of your associates?

So Nicodemus went to Jesus by night. He wanted to be a secret disciple, never called upon to defend publicly the faith he professed privately.

"Rabbi," he said, "we know that thou art a teacher come from God; for no one can do these signs that thou doest, except God be with him."

Jesus replied that "except a man be born again, he cannot see the kingdom of God."

These words puzzled the aging Nicodemus. He asked Jesus, "How can a man be born when he is old? Can he enter a second time into his mother's womb, and be born?"

Nicodemus, the man of discretion and worldly wisdom, did not understand the meaning of spiritual rebirth.

Later, when the chief priests and Pharisees gathered in council to plot Jesus' death, Nicodemus had only enough courage to suggest that, according to the law, no man should be judged without having an opportunity to defend himself.

But he quickly retreated into silence when the other members of the assembly turned on him. He was afraid to declare himself openly on the side of Jesus. He lacked the zeal and courage to use his influence to demand, rather than merely to suggest, justice.

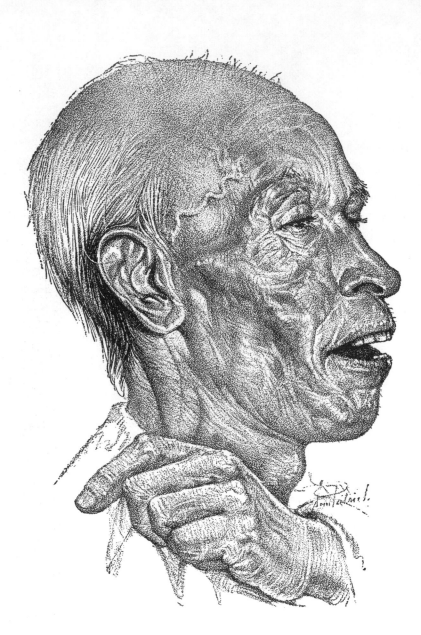

THE LEPER

"And, behold, there came a leper and worshipped him, saying, Lord, if thou wilt,
thou canst make me clean."

—*Matthew VIII:2*

WHEN JESUS healed the sick He used no strange nostrums, hocus-pocus, or histrionics that might enhance His reputation. His cures rested upon simple faith.

"Believe ye that I am able to do this?"

And when the suffering truly believed, as did this nameless leper, they were healed.

There is an apocryphal account of the conversation between this man of shining faith, and Jesus.

"Master, you are kind," he told Jesus. "And kindness is Truth, and Truth is God. I have found the meaning of this in the desert in a sudden shade, and in a cup of water. I have found it in the song long ago buried in my heart. But never before have I found it in a Man."

Jesus met the gaze of the sick man. Unlike others who drew away in repulsion and fear at his disfigured state, Jesus saw past the hideous mask of disease into the man's heart and soul. In the tortured face He saw trust and gladness.

"I understand thy loneliness," He answered, "for I, too, have known the rejection of men. My loneliness is sorrow that I cannot gather all into the Revelation of the Father's love, which I have known."

As Jesus spoke, the leper, exalted in his thoughts, memorized the line of His face and of His body. In a surge of faith, reinforced by love, he cried:

"Lord, if thou wilt, thou canst make me clean."

"And Jesus put forth his hand and touched him, saying, 'I will; be thou clean.' "

And the leper's affliction vanished. He was never again to suffer the anguish of the exiled and the defeated.

WOMAN OF SAMARIA

"There cometh a woman of Samaria to draw water: Jesus saith unto her, Give me to drink."

—*John IV:7*

J

ESUS WAS en route across Samaria, which lay between Judea and Galilee, when He paused at Jacob's well for refreshment, "being wearied with his journey."

The Samaritan woman was surprised at His request, because Jews held the Samaritans in contempt, and were forbidden to accept any favors from them.

But Jesus refused to recognize such religious and doctrinal barriers between people—barriers which made men enemies rather than brothers.

Jesus tells the Samaritan woman that if she knew the identity of the Traveler who had asked for a drink, she would have asked Him to give her to drink of living water.

But the woman does not immediately understand what He means by "living water." If He can get water without drawing it from the well, she says, then He must be greater than Jacob who established the well.

Jesus tells her: "Whosoever drinketh of this water shall thirst again: But whosoever drinketh of the water that I shall give him shall never thirst."

The woman still takes His words literally. She asks that He give her such a supply of water so she shall never have to come to the well to draw it.

Gradually, Jesus reveals to her the deeper meaning of His words. He shows His insight into her life and actions by showing her that He knows that she has had five husbands and is not married to him "whom thou now hast."

Then He discloses His true identity in the most explicit way: He is the Messiah she has heard will come.

At last the full import of the meeting with Jesus dawns on the woman. Forgetting the trivial task of the moment, she left her waterpot at the well and went into the city to tell the people of the "well of water springing up into everlasting life."

HEROD

"Now Herod the tetrarch heard of all that was done by him: and he was per-
plexed because that it was said of some, that John was risen from the dead."

—*Luke IX:7*

WHEN PILATE heard that Jesus was from Galilee, which came under the jurisdiction of Herod Antipas, he sent Him to Herod to be tried.

But the tetrarch, who already had the beheading of John the Baptist on his conscience, wanted nothing more to do with prophets, and sent Jesus back to Pilate.

He was a son of Herod the Great by one of the latter's five wives, Cleopatra, a native of Jerusalem. Reared amidst the intrigue of a corrupt court, he began his ruthless career at 17, when Augusta Caesar gave him as his share of his father's estate, the greater portion of Galilee.

When Tiberius Caesar became Emperor, Herod journeyed to Rome, where he sought to ingratiate himself with the ruler by offering his services as an informer, spying upon his own brothers, as well as upon Roman officials in Judea.

Although he was already married to the daughter of the Arabian king Aretas, during his voyage to Rome, he fell in love with Herodias, his niece by one brother, and the wife of another, and persuaded her, together with her daughter, to accompany him back to Galilee upon his return.

When John the Baptist also condemned Antipas for his incestuous union, Herodias persuaded the tetrarch to have John imprisoned, then, through her daughter, to have him beheaded.

After the death of Tiberius, Herod Antipas was sentenced to banishment by the new Emperor, Caligula, who had given a ready ear to accusations against Antipas, brought to Rome by the tetrarch's nephew, Agrippa Herod.

The manner of his death is not known, but the ancient Jewish historian, Josephus, indicates that he spent his last days in Spain.

He had ruled over Galilee for 43 years.

A CERTAIN YOUNG MAN

"And there followed him a certain young man, having a linen cloth cast about his naked body . . ."

—Mark XIV:51

scene of violence and infamy has just been enacted in the dark grove of olives.

When the mob of shouting, brutal men armed with swords and staves came to take Jesus, the disciples made a brief show of resistance. Simon Peter even drew his sword and cut off the ear of Malchus, servant to the high-priest.

But Jesus had told him, "Put up thy sword into the sheath: the cup which my Father hath given me, shall I not drink it?"

So the disciples have all fled to avoid arrest themselves.

The cruel henchmen of the temple priests have bound Jesus and are leading him towards the Holy City.

As the shameful band wends its way among the trees, their shadows grotesque and ugly in the flickering light of lanterns, one of the guards bringing up the rear looks back.

Following the Messiah's captors is a young man with only a linen wrap about him.

Who is he, this mysterious youth who has not taken time to dress? Does he live in a house nearby, awakened by all the commotion in the grove, and has come to investigate?

Is it because he is a friend of Jesus that he follows Him through this hour of darkness toward the final road to Calvary?

Or is it merely curiosity that has made him an unintentional witness of the first act in the bloody drama that is to follow?

Mark, the only one of the Evangelists to refer to him, does not say.

But it is evident that the guards believe him to be one of the followers of Jesus who has not fled. So they seize him by his linen wrapper, but he escapes and disappears stark nude into the darkness of the grove.

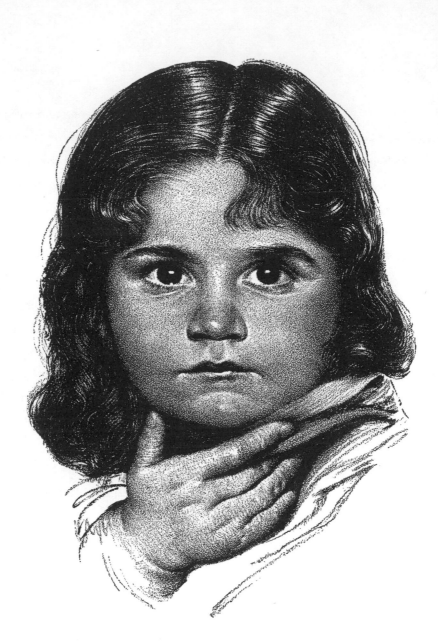

CHILD IN THE MIDST

"And Jesus called a little child unto him, and set him in the midst of them."

—*Matthew XVIII:2*

THERE WERE always children about Jesus, chattering in happiness and darting through the crowds to His side, as the birds in the garden of Gethsemane that often punctuated His thoughts.

The grown men who had chosen to follow in the way of the Nazarene tried always to shoo them away, for their young minds did not dwell on the words of Jesus; but their hearts were glad in His presence.

And time after time Jesus rebuked His followers, saying:

"Suffer little children, and forbid them not, to come unto me: for of such is the kingdom of heaven."

So, calling this child to Him, Jesus smiled down into the bright eyes of trust, as He caressed the wind-freed hair. And looking up into the face of the kind man from Judea, the child listened strangely to His words, as if entranced.

"Verily I say unto you, Except ye be converted, and become as little children, ye shall not enter into the kingdom of heaven."

To some men God is a possession, to others a desire. To some He is a benefactor, a judge, or a tyrant. But always the God of man is the will of man.

To a child in its innocence and in its feeling, God is the rustle of a mother's skirt in the dream-troubled darkness, and her soothing hands. He is the promise of awakening after the night's sleep, the radiant happiness of a gift—a new toy.

In a word, for the child God is love. And only through love, the Evangelist tells us, can we know God.

Still regarding the large eyes fastened upon His own with a quiet confidence, Jesus told his disciples:

"Whosoever therefore shall humble himself as this little child, the same is greatest in the kingdom of heaven."

ANNA THE PROPHETESS

"And there was one Anna, a prophetess, the daughter of Phanuel, of the tribe of Aser: she was of a great age . . ."

—*Luke II:36*

ALTHOUGH THE Scripture refers to this pious widow as a "prophetess," it is clear from the context that she was a mystic in the better sense of the word, rather than a mere soothsayer.

Like Jacob, from whom her tribe claimed descent, she struggled with the mysteries of God, seeking an understanding beyond man's world.

Even though she was eighty-four years old, her advanced age had not dimmed her spiritual vision. Rather, she had quickened it by "fastings and prayers night and day."

There were many who had a greater knowledge of the Scriptures than she—the Scribes and publicans, and Pharisees. But among them there were few who loved God more. And, as Pascal has observed, "How far it is from the knowledge of God to a love of Him!"

Because of her devotion and constant attendance at the Temple, she entered just as Simeon uttered his moving prayer of thanks to God for the privilege of holding in his arms the Salvation of the world.

And she "gave thanks likewise unto the Lord, and spake of him to all them that looked for redemption in Jerusalem."

How was it, we may ask, that both Simeon and Anna instantly recognized in the small bundle that Mary held in her arms, the supernatural power and majesty of the awaited King of Kings?

Was it a happy coincidence, a bit of fortunate guesswork on the part of two wishful thinkers who had dwelt overlong on the words and promise of the prophets?

No; the Evangelist makes it clear in his brief account that Anna and Simeon had prepared themselves by devotion, fastings and prayer to know God when He appeared before them.

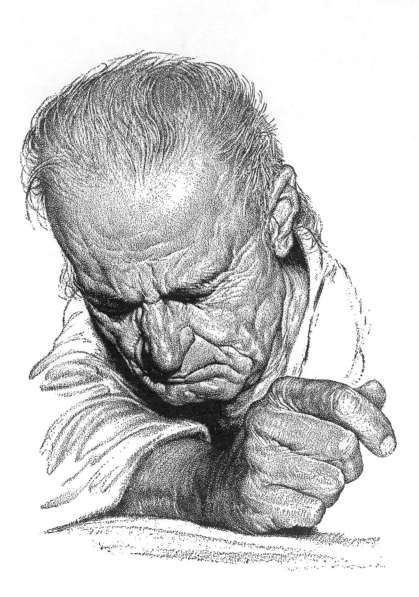

THE DEAF MAN

"And they bring unto him one that was deaf, and had an impediment in his speech; and they beseech him to put his hand upon him."

—*Mark VII: 32*

I

N ADDITION to being deaf, this man had the misfortune to be tongue-tied or perhaps altogether dumb, for after he was healed, the astonished crowd commented:

"He maketh both the deaf to hear and the dumb to speak."

Aside from a detailed description of the unusual manner in which Jesus accomplished the cure, the Gospel narrative does not take the space to recount anything about the deaf man himself.

There is, however, a beautiful tradition about this mute whose deep awareness and trust in Jesus were rewarded with the gift of restored hearing and speech.

This man had lived his years in silence, yet intent upon enjoying the beauties within his power to understand. He delighted in the touch of things.

With delicate skill, his fingers shaped his thoughts into communication with his fellow men through the medium of sculpture.

But often his thoughts dwelt upon his plight: "I am a man, but I am not as other men. So I will weave a language of my thoughts in other ways."

So he carved of stone and wood faces that expressed the emotion of his thoughts. So skilled was he that his eye detected in every face the inner mask which he named: "the mask of thought."

While he studied men for impressions of human nature, he sought an understanding of his own. All of this prepared him to recognize in Jesus the answer to his yearnings.

So in finding Him, the mute man expected to find also the powers of response with which to express his gratitude. And this he did.

For years later, in a foreign land, he sculptured at the request of Mary Magdalene a likeness of Jesus.

ZACCHAEUS

"And behold, there was a man named Zacchaeus, which was the chief among the publicans, and he was rich."

—Luke XIX:2

As JESUS passed through the city of Jericho, He was surrounded by the crowds who always gathered at His appearance—the idly curious, the spiritual seekers, the enemies of Truth.

Among the multitude this day was the wealthy tax collector, Zacchaeus. From the title, "chief among the publicans," it is clear that he was in charge of public revenues in his district.

Any person with such a job has never been popular. Owing to the fact that in the time of Christ, tax collectors were often dishonest, anyone who held the office was disliked by the people.

It is not surprising, therefore, that when Zacchaeus, who was very short of stature, eagerly sought to see Jesus, the crowd did not make way for him.

Determined to look upon the Master, Zacchaeus ran ahead of the crowd that pressed Jesus as He moved down the street, and climbed a sycamore tree.

"And when Jesus came to the place, he looked up, and saw him, and said unto him, Zacchaeus, make haste and come down; for today I must abide at thy house."

The bystanders, who a few moments before had prevented Zacchaeus from getting a glimpse of the Savior, now criticized Jesus for accepting hospitality from a sinner.

Zacchaeus, for his part, hastened to tell Jesus:

"Lord, the half of my goods I give to the poor; and if I have taken any thing from any man by false accusation, I restore him fourfold."

And Jesus, who saw within the hearts of men and knew their thoughts, ignored the protests of the crowd. He told Zacchaeus:

"This day is salvation come to this house, forsomuch as he also is a son of Abraham. For the Son of man is come to seek and to save that which was lost."

BLIND MAN OF BETHSAIDA

"And he cometh to Bethsaida; and they bring a blind man unto him, and besought him to touch him."

—*Mark VIII:22*

I N AFFLICTION, a man may sometimes turn away from his surface confusions to seek the calm of inner thought.

So it was with this unfortunate man of Bethsaida, who had, as a 19th century writer once described blindness, "in the school of darkness learned what mean 'the things unseen.'"

To avoid the observation of the critical and unbelieving populace, Jesus led the blind man by the hand outside the town.

There He anointed the sightless eyes with spittle, "and put his hands upon him."

"Seest thou ought?" the Savior then asked.

And, struggling toward light, which seemed as yet so faint and far off, the blind man answered:

"I see men as trees, walking."

So Jesus once more laid His gentle and healing hands upon the undiscerning eyes, and told the man again to look up.

Gradually, as he strained to see, the moving shadows beyond his pit of darkness took shape and he saw a radiant nimbus that became a Face.

Then other faces came into focus: the visages that reflected the wonder and awe of the disciples who had witnessed miracles before, but each time stared as men awakened from a dream.

But it was the Face of God that his restored vision first beheld that would henceforth be the polestar of this man's life.

He wanted to shout for joy, to announce the miracle of his restoration in every street and in the market place of the wicked town.

But Jesus told him instead to return to his home, saying, "Neither go into the town, nor tell it to any in the town."

JOSEPH OF ARIMATHAEA

"And, behold, there was a man named Joseph, a counseller; and he was a good man, and a just: (The same had not consented to the counsel and deed of them;) he was of Arimathaea, a city of the Jews . . ."

—Luke XXIII:50,51

J OSEPH, LIKE Nicodemus, another member of the Jewish Great Council or Sanhedrin, was a secret disciple of Jesus.

St. Luke calls him a good and just man, who refused to consent to the verdict of the Sanhedrin when they condemned Jesus.

Although he may not have openly challenged the verdict, he did show more courage than the Nazarene's own disciples when, on the very evening of the Crucifixion, he "went boldly unto Pilate and craved the body of Jesus."

Pilate was surprised to learn that Jesus was already dead. Crucified men often lingered in agony on the cross for two days. The Procurator called in the centurion who had been in charge of the execution for a report. Learning that Jesus had indeed expired on the Cross, he gave Joseph permission to take down His body.

Papini points out that Pilate thus disregarded a Roman custom of the day, according to which Roman officers who were in charge of executions could collect a fee from families or friends of the crucified for delivery of the body.

Josephus and Nicodemus, attended by Mary Magdalene and probably the other two Marys, took the body of Jesus to a garden in which the wealthy Joseph had had a sepulchre for himself hewn in a rock.

There the sacred body was prepared for burial: washed, sprinkled with spices, wrapped in a linen shroud, and a napkin placed over the face.

Then, by the eerie, flickering light of torches, the white-shrouded body was laid in the tomb and a great rock rolled against the opening to seal it up.

Here in the chill blackness of death He was to remain until the dawn of Easter, when from the dark night of man's pit-world the radiance of Resurrection rolled aside the stone and flooded the world with the light of immortality.

TWO FALSE WITNESSES

"At the last came two false witnesses, And said, This fellow said, I am able to destroy the temple of God, and to build it in three days."

—*Matthew XXVI:60,61*

At the preliminary hearing before the high priest Caiaphas, "the chief priests, and elders, and all the council, sought false witness against Jesus, to put him to death."

There were many such false witnesses, all perfectly willing to give perjured testimony against the Man of Galilee.

But most of them could not serve that evil end, even though they desired to do so. The reason was two-fold:

First, the Council wanted a charge against Jesus that would be so serious in nature that it would both demand the Roman governor's attention and at the same time call for the death sentence.

Second, according to the Mosaic law, it was necessary that two witnesses, when examined separately, with the other not present, both testify to the same details of evidence against the accused.

At last the Council found two men who no doubt had agreed outside upon what each would say.

Sly, stoop-shouldered and wrapped in their mantles like vultures, they shifted their weight uneasily from one foot to the other and blinked puffy eyelids as they stared into the bright flames of the lamps.

So they maliciously lied: "This fellow said, I am able to destroy the temple of God, and to build it in three days."

This statement was, of course, a perversion of the Savior's allusion to His coming death, the destruction of His bodily temple, which He would again raise from the dead on the third day.

But twisted to mean a threat against the Temple of Jerusalem, it was blasphemy—a capital offense to the Jews—and sedition, a crime meriting death in Roman eyes.

CLEOPAS

"And one of them, whose name was Cleopas, answering said unto him, Art thou only a stranger in Jerusalem . . .?"

—Luke XXIV:18

IT WAS on the day of Jesus' resurrection that Cleopas and another follower of Jesus set out from Jerusalem for Emmaus, a village lying seven or eight miles to the west.

Just before their departure, John and Peter had returned from the empty tomb. The report that Jesus had risen from the dead excited them, but it was not immediately accepted as truth.

As Cleopas and his unnamed companion disputed with each other over the wisdom of once again believing in what was apparently a lost cause, they were overtaken by a Wayfarer.

After a brief greeting, the Stranger walked with them down the road toward Emmaus. Politely, he asked the subject of their dispute.

Cleopas answered, "Art thou only a stranger in Jerusalem, and hast not known the things which are come to pass in these days?"

"What things?" asked their unknown Companion of the way.

So Cleopas poured out the story of the Crucifixion and of their own bewilderment, and the report that He had risen that morning from the dead.

Chiding them for being so dull spiritually, the Stranger then explained to them the meaning of the Scriptural prophecies concerning the Messiah.

But, although they marveled at His knowledge and insight, they still did not recognize Him. Still, He was a wonderful conversationalist, and they begged Him to spend the night with them.

As they sat down to supper, "he took the bread, and blessed it, and brake, and gave to them."

As He performed this ritual, so reminiscent of the Last Supper just three days previously, "their eyes were opened, and they knew him."

And Jesus, having restored their spiritual sight, vanished.

LEGION—MAN OF THE TOMBS

"And when he was come out of the ship, immediately there met him out of the tombs a man with an unclean spirit . . ."

—*Mark V:2*

I<small>N HIS ACCOUNT</small> of this incident, Matthew mentions two men possessed with devils. But both Mark and Luke refer to only one.

It may be that the latter evangelists allude only to the demoniac whose case was much more unusual than that of the other.

He was possessed not of just one unclean spirit, but of so many that his name was Legion. The term, which designated a subdivision of the Roman army, numbering about 6,000 men, in common speech meant any large number.

The Gospel says "he had often been bound with fetters and chains, and the chains had been plucked asunder by him, and the fetters broken in pieces: neither could any man tame him." Such strength is clearly more than that of a madman; it suggests the supernatural power of Satan.

As in other Gospel accounts of possession, the evil spirits which had usurped this man's body recognized Jesus "from afar off."

Fearing the power of Jesus, the demoniac cried: "I adjure thee by God that thou torment me not."

Curiously, the devils did not want to leave the district in which they had exercised their evil powers. Instead, "they besought him, saying, Send us into the swine, that we may enter into them."

There were about two thousand of the animals in the herd, apparently kept by the Gadarenes in violation of the Jewish religious law.

Jesus did not command the unclean spirits to enter the swine; he "gave them leave." And they ran down a steep slope and were drowned in the sea.

And Legion, now fully clothed and in his right mind, begged that he might go with Jesus. But the Savior told him: "Go home to thy friends, and tell them how great things the Lord hath done for thee."

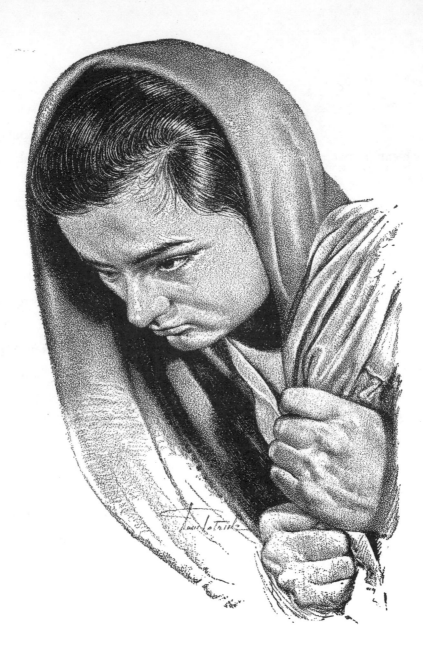

MARTHA

"But Martha was cumbered about much serving, and came to him, and said, Lord, dost thou not care that my sister hath left me to serve alone?"

—*Luke X:40*

MARTHA, THE SISTER of Lazarus and Mary, who lived in the village of Bethany, personifies the kind of devotion that expresses itself in service.

Because she loved Jesus, she wanted more than anything else to minister to His physical needs.

So the moment the Master crosses the threshold of her house, she rushes about to see that He is comfortable and well fed. He is surely tired from his journey, and would like to wash. He must have a good meal, too, and refreshment.

She sets about at once with household chores—lighting the fire, preparing food, laying the table.

When her sister Mary does not stir a hand to assist her, but merely sits at Jesus' feet, transfixed as she listens to His every word, Martha complains to Jesus.

It seems to her that if Mary loved Jesus as she does, she would surely want to serve Him. But Jesus tells her:

"Martha, Martha, thou art careful and troubled about many things: but one thing is needful: and Mary hath chosen that good part, which shall not be taken away from her."

Nevertheless, Jesus understood Martha's attitude, and He loved her for her devotion and response to Him.

Later, at the Passover Supper in Bethany, after her brother has been raised from the dead by Jesus, it is still Martha who serves the table.

But, from the brief glimpse we have of her on this occasion, it is clear that she has been freed from her former preoccupation with household cares. She is no longer cumbered, no longer "troubled about many things." For her devotion has led her to a realization of "the one thing that is needful"—love made calm with trust.

MARY SISTER OF MARTHA

"And she had a sister called Mary, which also sat at Jesus' feet, and heard his word."

—*Luke* X:39

M

ARY, THE SISTER of Martha, is sometimes called the Contemplative Mary because of her deep, meditative devotion in the presence of Jesus.

She lived with her sister and her brother Lazarus in Bethany, a village about two miles outside Jerusalem. All three were intimate friends of Jesus who showed a great affection for them, and often visited in their home with His disciples.

When Martha called upon Jesus to rebuke Mary because the latter sat listening to the Master's every word while Martha prepared supper, Jesus explained that Mary had chosen the good part, the "one thing needful."

Six days before the Passover, Jesus came to Bethany with His disciples and was, as usual, invited to supper. Present at the table, in addition to Martha and Mary, was Lazarus, whom Jesus had raised from the dead.

Grateful to Jesus for His love, and perhaps sensing that the time of separation was near, Mary expressed her affection and respect in a dramatic way.

She took "a pound of ointment of spikenard, very costly, and anointed the feet of Jesus, and wiped his feet with her hair: and the house was filled with the odour of the ointment."

Judas Iscariot muttered that this seemed a waste of money that could have been given to the poor. But Jesus silenced him with the words:

"Let her alone: against the day of my burying hath she kept this. For the poor always ye have with you; but me ye have not always."

Most Catholic authorities hold that the sinner mentioned in Luke VII:36-50, Mary the sister of Martha, and Mary Magdalene are all the same person.

The Greek Fathers and later Protestant scholars do not agree, but distinguish the three.

MAN WITH A WITHERED HAND

"And, behold, there was a man which had his hand withered . . ."

—*Matthew XII:10*

THIS MAN's affliction is believed to have been a form of catalepsy. As it was known in the time of Jesus, the disease first manifested itself by the contraction of the muscles in some part of the body, often the hand or arm.

The onset was usually quite sudden. After the seizure, the victim's hand gradually grew smaller in size, and assumed a dried-up appearance. For that reason it was called "a withered hand."

It was a far more serious disease than is apparent merely from this reference to it. Medical authorities believe it was a progressive form of paralysis. After invading one limb, it spread slowly to other parts of the body.

This was the kind of creeping death that faced the man who was among the Pharisees in the synagogue that sabbath day when Jesus entered.

The Gospel story does not tell us whether the afflicted man asked Jesus to heal him. It is quite likely, however, that he did. Perhaps he had even followed Jesus to the synagogue, with the idea of asking the Galilean to cure his dread malady.

How, he may have wondered, can tissue already destroyed, be restored? Were the stories he had heard true—that this Man of miracles could heal all ills by a mere gesture, a look, a command?

Then he looked into the face of Jesus. He remarked the love, compassion and power in the deep eyes. And suddenly a feeling flooded his whole being, a feeling that sets aside all else in its recognition of the Real. In his consciousness there was no hidden reserve, no question, no doubt. He believed.

And in the presence of the Pharisees who hoped to trap Him in an unlawful act, Jesus told the sick man: "Stretch forth thine hand."

And he stretched it forth "and it was restored whole, like as the other."

THE SHEPHERD

"And it came to pass as the angels were gone away from them into heaven, the shepherds said one to another, Let us now go even unto Bethlehem, and see this thing which is come to pass . . ."

—*Luke II:15*

I F JESUS had been born in a palace instead of a stable, there would have been something incongruous in the visit of Judean shepherds to his birthplace.

The Gospels do not tell us what became of those shepherds in the years that followed. But there is a legend still told in Bible lands concerning one of the shepherds named Abishai. It goes like this:

After waiting for the last note of the angels' jubilant melody—borne upon a breeze blowing from distant reaches of light—Abishai said to his companions:

"Let us hasten to the City of David and see for ourselves this thing the Lord has made known unto us."

As they prepared to depart, Abishai drove his shepherd's staff deeply into the earth of the hillside to mark the spot where the winged minstrels had appeared. It was his plan to build a shrine where all of the shepherds might come and give thanks to the Creator for the message to them. But it was the will of God that Abishai was not to see his familiar hillside again for a long time.

For, finding the Infant Jesus as the angel had promised, and feeling within himself the true meaning of His birth into man's world of shadows, Abishai set forth to carry the tidings to the whole country.

During the years that followed, the staff, planted in the earth at the spot of annunciation, took root and grew into a flowering thorn tree.

When Jesus grew to manhood and journeyed this way during His ministry, He paused to rest in the shade of the tree. There Abishai, who had finally returned to his homeland, met again the Infant who was now a Man. "Why comest thou hither?" Jesus asked him.

"To find Him whom the angels announced to me on the night of His birth," Abishai replied. Jesus told him: "Find me in thy will to follow where I lead."

And he smiled upon the shepherd, who could not speak.

THE SCRIBE

"And a certain scribe came, and said unto him, Master, I will follow thee wither-soever thou goest."

—Matthew VIII:19

Jesus was a brilliant expounder of the Scriptures; He performed many miracles; His influence over the people was evident in the multitudes who followed Him wherever He went.

It was no doubt for these reasons that this scribe wished to join His group of intimate followers. Perhaps he thought he might learn the secret of the Nazarene's power, and share in His honors and gain.

Whatever his motive, it is evident that it was not a sincere desire to follow in the steps of the Master or to know God better.

As a matter of fact, the scribes were almost without exception the enemies of Jesus. They were known as scribes because they transcribed the Mosaic law, and wrote commentaries upon it. Most of them were Pharisees, zealous adherents to traditions.

But they considered themselves a superior class, proud of their own learning, which was but a reflection of the true word of God.

Jesus knew what was in this scribe's heart. He knew that his declaration, "I will follow thee whithersoever thou goest," could not be taken literally and unconditionally.

Would the scribe, whose life was spent in refining upon and corrupting the law of God, now push aside his vanity and his self-interest for the homeless poverty of a true disciple?

Jesus reminded him of what his decision would mean:

"The foxes have holes, and the birds of the air have nests; but the son of man hath not where to lay his head."

Although Matthew does not bother to tell us implicitly what the scribe's reaction to these words was, it is plain from his background and from the context:

He instantly lost interest in becoming a disciple.

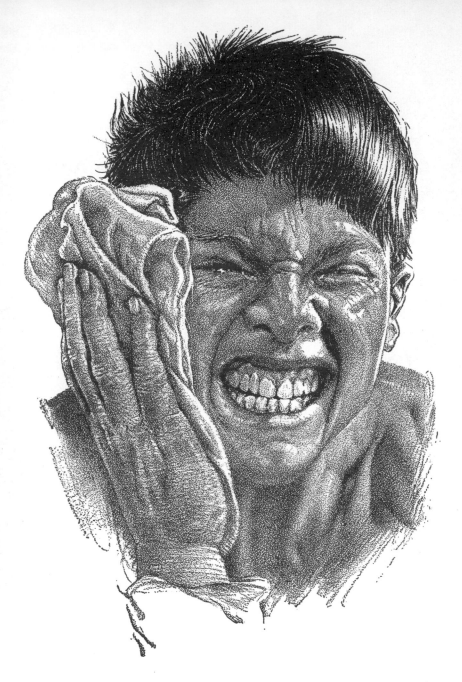

SERVANT OF THE HIGH PRIEST

*"And, behold, one of them which were with Jesus stretched out his hand, and
drew his sword, and struck a servant of the high priest's, and smote off his ear."*

—*Matthew XXVI:51*

J OHN TELLS US in his Gospel that Malchus was the name of this hireling who was among those sent by Caiaphas to arrest Jesus.

The Evangelist also identifies the disciple who impulsively resorted to violence against the mob from the Temple. It was Simon Peter, the brawny fisherman. Although he was only one against a multitude, so great was his indignation that he struck out with his sword, slicing off the right ear of Malchus.

It is, in fact, surprising to find one of Jesus' disciples armed, for He had repeatedly told them that they should not resist the persecutions of men, "but whosoever shall smite thee on thy right cheek, turn to him the other also."

Yet the growing opposition to Jesus by the Temple authorities, the whispered plots, the glib secret agents sent to spy on the Nazarene and His followers —all this had made the disciples a little jumpy and apprehensive.

They wanted to believe in the Lord's assurances and in His admonition to "love your enemies, bless them that curse you, do good to them that hate you," but the primitive instinct of self-preservation was too strong.

Jesus instantly halted Peter's courageous but futile outburst.

"Put up again thy sword into its place," He told the angry disciple. "For all they that take the sword shall perish with the sword."

If He needed protection, Jesus said, He could pray to the Father "and he shall presently give me more than twelve legions of angels."

No; the tragic and final drama begun in this hour of darkness had to run its course to the final shocking denouement on the Hill of Skulls. But the meaning of it was not death, but a victory over death, and eternal life for men.

So, gently the Savior restored the servant's severed ear, and held out His hands for His captors' chains.

THE PALSIED MAN

"And they come unto him, bringing one sick of the palsy, which was borne by four."

—*Mark II:3*

THE TEACHING and miracles of Jesus had aroused such widespread interest among the people that when He returned to Capernaum, crowds thronged to the house where He was staying.

As Jesus was addressing them, this paralytic, so sorely afflicted that he had to be carried by four friends, approached the house.

They implored the dense crowd to part and allow the sick man passage into the presence of the Galilean. But to no avail. No one would yield his place.

After a whispered consultation with his friends, he was carried up the outside stairway of the house to the flat roof. There his friends set to work removing the tiles, flat stones and hardened clay until they had opened a hole large enough to lower the infirm man into the room below.

There Jesus greeted him with a gentle smile. And looking deep into the suffering eyes, where He beheld the cause of the palsied man's illness, He said:

"Son, thy sins be forgiven thee."

Like the able and experienced physician that He was, Jesus knew that the root of this man's affliction was in his mind and his heart. But even though he had sinned, his faith could make him whole again.

"Blasphemy!" thought the Pharisees who were present. "Who can forgive sins except God?" And Jesus, knowing their thoughts, asked them, "Wherefore think ye evil in your hearts? For whether is it easier, to say, Thy sins be forgiven thee; or to say, Arise and walk?"

Anyone, it was true, could claim to forgive sins. But who could back up such absolution with a miracle that proved it? Jesus did, at once. Turning back to the palsied man, He told him: "Arise, take up thy bed and go unto thine house." And, fully restored, the man did just that.

MAID OF THE HIGH PRIEST

"Then said the damsel that kept the door unto Peter, Art not thou also one of this man's disciples? He saith, I am not."

—*John XVIII:17*

Two of Jesus' disciples followed at a safe distance as His captors led Him through the dark streets of Jerusalem to the house of the high priest.

After the Savior had been taken inside, one of the disciples—almost certainly John—knocked at the door and asked to be admitted. .

The maid who kept the door recognized him and allowed him to enter. But his companion, who was Simon Peter, remained outside—either through fear or because he did not think he would be permitted to enter.

When Peter did not follow him inside, however, John spoke to the girl who kept the door, vouching for his companion and asking her to let him come in.

The maid went out and brought Peter inside. In the vestibule (called a porch), just inside the doorway leading to the street, she asked Peter:

"Art not thou also one of this man's disciples?"

"I am not," said Peter indignantly.

From the way the maid had worded her question, it would appear that she was merely making sure of Peter's identity rather than accusing him of being a disciple.

Was this the same disciple who a short time before had drawn his sword and was ready to fight the whole mob who had come to take Jesus?

His heated denials—to the maid of the high priest, to the others who challenged him, and to the relative of Malchus, whose ear he had cut off—all these seem wholly inconsistent with Peter's courage in the Garden.

But the maid of the high priest did not know this, any more than she knew that the minor role she played in that night's grim drama had endowed her with a kind of immortality, however slight it is.

THE GOOD THIEF

"And he said unto Jesus, Lord, remember me when thou comest into thy kingdom."
—Luke XXIII:42

TWO HARDENED CRIMINALS are paying the ultimate price for their careers of lawlessness—nailed to the cross.

Between them on a third cross hangs the Gentle Shepherd of men's lives, "numbered among the transgressors."

Even during the throes of his own final agony, one of the thieves reflects the mockery and scorn of the crowd. Twisting his head toward Jesus, he cries:

"If thou be the Christ, save thyself and us."

But his companion, who had listened in astonishment as the Man on the cross between them had said, "Father forgive them; for they know not what they do," now felt a new response and love for the Nazarene flood his whole being. He found within himself an awakening which cleared his thoughts to a change of perspective.

And that change of perspective called into expression a discerning and elevated consciousness. Enlightment thus developed the thoughts of this dying malefactor until the negative impression of his first reaction to Jesus was changed to a true understanding. Forgetting his own agony, he turned upon his fellow thief.

"Dost thou not fear God," he said, "seeing thou art in the same condemnation? And we indeed justly; for we receive the due reward for our deeds: but this man hath done nothing amiss."

Perhaps in that terrible moment of suffering, mixed with pity for the innocent Man who suffered so great an injustice and the profound recognition of that Man's identity, the Good Thief sensed the coming Resurrection, for he cried: "Lord, remember me when thou comest into thy kingdom."

And Jesus, who was to know, even in the darkest hour of man's rejection, man's trust and man's faith, answered:

"Verily, I say unto thee, today shalt thou be with me in paradise."

THE BAD THIEF

"And one of the malefactors which were hanged railed on him, saying, If thou be Christ, save thyself and us."

—*Luke XXIII:39*

EVEN IN HIS DEATH THROES, the "bad" thief—Jesus' companion in agony—reviled Him, echoing the mockery of the mob.

But the other thief, recognizing Jesus and trusting in His promise of a life to come, rebuked his unrepentant cohort:

"Dost thou not fear God, seeing thou art in the same condemnation? And we indeed justly; for we receive the due reward of our deeds: but this man hath done nothing amiss."

But, although this may have silenced the unregenerate man's jeers, it apparently did not persuade him that Jesus was indeed the Redeemer.

This story of the two thieves vividly illustrates the duality of man. His nobler nature—his soul—responds to Truth with the humble request:

"Lord, remember me when thou comest into thy kingdom."

But his mortal, physical mind, with its accumulation of evil thoughts, rejects the good.

The words of forgiveness, uttered by the dying Jesus, found no echo in the heart of the bad thief. Only bitter selfishness and resentment that this Man who claimed to be the Messiah could not save Himself, and His two companions along with Him.

But He could not even ease His own suffering. The insults flung up at Him by the crowd were justified. He was a fraud, the bad thief thought.

Jesus was ready with forgiveness even in the final hour of His earthly life. It was His plan that even the least among men—even a thief—might inherit the kingdom of God.

For no man who lifted up his yearning to Him was denied an answer.

But the bad thief did not ask for that kind of salvation. And thus he closed the door on everlasting life.

RICH YOUNG MAN

"And, behold, one came and said unto him, Good Master, what thing shall I do, that I may have eternal life?"

—*Matthew XIX:16*

THE WEALTHY YOUNG RULER who asked Jesus this question was sincere so far as seeking moral perfection was concerned.

He proudly told the Savior that he had kept the moral commandments of Moses from his youth up. "What lack I yet?"

His greatest need, Jesus said, was the kind of faith that will forsake earthly possessions to follow Him.

"If thou wilt be perfect, go and sell that thou hast, and give to the poor, and thou shalt have treasure in heaven: and come and follow me."

Proceed even as I, he told the young man. Live to grow. Work and follow the pattern of each day's guidance. Care for thy needs, but do not hold the wheel of the Spinner (who weaves the tapestry of men's lives).

Then, verily, a loaf is as a thousand loaves, and a single fish feeds many. For bounty is release from all stagnant holdings in the mind that this release be extended into the material experience of men.

But the young man could not grasp this. What was his personal guarantee of such a supply?

Jesus' own life held the answer: there is no assurance but trust in the guidance of thy feet, and in the work of thy hands, and in the belief that is love for the Father.

If thy purse be empty, yet it shall be filled to thy need. But if the heart be empty, it is as a bottomless pit.

I give thee that by which thou canst restore thyself to a place among the living.

"Come and follow me!"

"But when the young man heard that saying, he went away sorrowful, for he had great possessions."

FIRST WISE MAN

". . . Behold, there came wise men from the east to Jerusalem."

—*Matthew II:1*

O<small>NLY</small> M<small>ATTHEW</small> among the four Gospel writers mentions the Magi and their journey to Bethlehem. And he does not tell us how many there were, what they were called, or exactly which countries they were from.

In the West, tradition has always indicated that there were three such Wise Men. This number is probably based upon the fact that Matthew mentions three gifts, which they brought to the Child Jesus. In the East, on the other hand, legends say there were twelve.

The legends of different countries have given the Wise Men various names. But the three most familiar to the West, from the seventh century onward, are Melchior, Gaspar, and Balthasar.

An early writer even ventures a description of the three. He says that Melchior, the First Wise Man, was "an old man, grey-haired, with a long, full beard. He came bearing a gift of gold to the princely Infant."

But exactly who was this hoary man of learning, and what was the nature of his knowledge that even in a distant country he could discern what apparently remained hidden from all save the shepherds among the people in the immediate vicinity of the event in the Bethlehem stable?

Non-Biblical sources tell us that originally the Magi were a sect of Medes who worshipped God in the emblem of fire. Later, however, the name was applied to followers of the Persian reformer, Zoroaster, who restored the Magian system and introduced into it the principle of one supreme God.

The sect, members of which collected together in colleges, or centers of learning, were profound students of astrology, and were skilled in the interpretation of dreams.

As stargazers who constantly studied the heavens, it is not surprising that they noted "his star in the east" and set out to find Him.

SECOND WISE MAN

". . . We have seen his star in the east, and are come to worship him."

—Matthew II:2

ACCORDING to the Venerable Bede, seventh century English writer, the second wise man was named Kaspar (sometimes also spelled Gaspar).

He is described as having been a beardless youth, with light hair and ruddy complexion. His gift to the Child was frankincense, a fragrant gum which, when placed on hot coals, produces an aromatic vapor.

The exact time at which the Magi arrived to present their offerings and to worship the new Messiah is not given us by Matthew.

Some writers have expressed the view that the wise men did not reach Bethlehem on the night Jesus was born, but probably a year or so later.

Others reason that it may have been as long as two years, since Herod, when the wise men did not return to tell him whether they had indeed found an Infant King, slew all male children under two.

But such a conclusion could easily be wrong. It is possible that the Magi deceived him about the time the star appeared.

And was it really a star, after all? Was it, as rationalists would have us believe today, a natural configuration of heavenly bodies that happened to coincide with the time of Christ's birth? Was it a comet, blazing a trail across the sky? A meteor plummeting to earth in the dark Judean hills?

Clearly not, if the Evangelist speaks the truth. For he writes that the star "went before them, till it came and stood over where the young child was."

Rather, it is more like the pillar of fire which guided the people of Israel during their wanderings in the desert wilderness. And why should these men of the East follow this new star to find a king of the Jews? The most likely explanation is that they were familiar with the general expectation that a divine Redeemer would be born in Palestine.

THIRD WISE MAN

"And being warned of God in a dream that they should not return to Herod, they departed into their own country another way."

—*Matthew II:12*

O PINIONS VARY as to the national origins of the wise men. The fact that they came from east of Jerusalem seems to point to Persia. Supporting this view is also the fact that Persia was the country where the Magi conducted their schools or center of occult learning.

But men from throughout the East went to Persia to study with those teachers and adepts to be found there. So the wise men might, indeed, have represented different countries.

Bede states that the third wise man, Balthasar, was dark-skinned and bearded. He was, according to this account, an African, probably from Arabia, since the gift he presented to Jesus was myrrh. This highly-fragrant substance, valued as a perfume, came from a small tree or shrub native to Arabia.

(It is interesting to note that myrrh figures in both the birth and the death of the Savior. As the wise man's gift, it was an "oil of gladness," offered in homage to the newborn king. As He suffered upon the cross, he was offered the same substance, mingled with wine to alleviate his pain, but He rejected it.)

On their journey to Bethlehem, the Magi probably traveled a distance of slightly more than 1,000 miles, requiring from three to nine months by camel.

They probably followed the great caravan route across the Syrian desert with its scorching winds, to the oasis of Tadmor (Palmyra), and on to Damascus, then southward until they forded the Jordan near Jericho. They returned by some other and probably more circuitous route.

Scripture, unfortunately, does not tell us what became of these spiritually enlightened men of the East in the years that followed.

According to tradition, they were later baptized by the Apostle Thomas. In the Cathedral at Cologne are relics said to be the remains of the wise men which St. Helena had discovered in Persia.

SIMEON

"And, behold, there was a man named in Jerusalem, whose name was Simeon;
and the same man was just and devout, waiting for the consolation of Israel . . ."

—*Luke II:25*

LIKE MOST DEVOUT JEWS of his day, Simeon had long awaited the coming of the Messiah who would deliver Israel from alien domination, and usher in a new age.

In long nights of prayer and vigil, he meditated upon the words of the Prophets, who had foretold the advent of the Anointed One:

Daniel, who had pointed to an exact time and place of His arrival. Haggai and Malachi, who had said that He would appear before the destruction of the Second Temple in Jerusalem. Micah, who foretold that He would be born in Bethlehem; and Isaiah, who predicted a virgin birth.

"O Lord," prayed Simeon, fearing that his life was drawing to its close, "let me not see death until I have looked upon the Deliverer."

And wisdom's single eye, which pierced the mind's dark veils, looked upon a vision which revealed to Simeon the fulfillment of his desire.

So he followed the guidance extended him "by the Spirit," and entered the Temple that day as Joseph and Mary came with the Infant Jesus "to do for him after the custom of the law."

When he looked into the radiance of the Child's face, the joy of recognition leaped like a flame in Simeon's breast. And with the parents' consent, the old man "took him up in his arms, and blessed God, and said:

"Lord, now lettest thou thy servant depart in peace, according to thy word: for mine eyes have seen thy salvation, which thou hast prepared before the face of all people."

This beautiful hymn—thanksgiving for rewarded faith—was to be repeated ever after by those who had caught a glimpse of the same radiance in the long twilight of their mortal years.

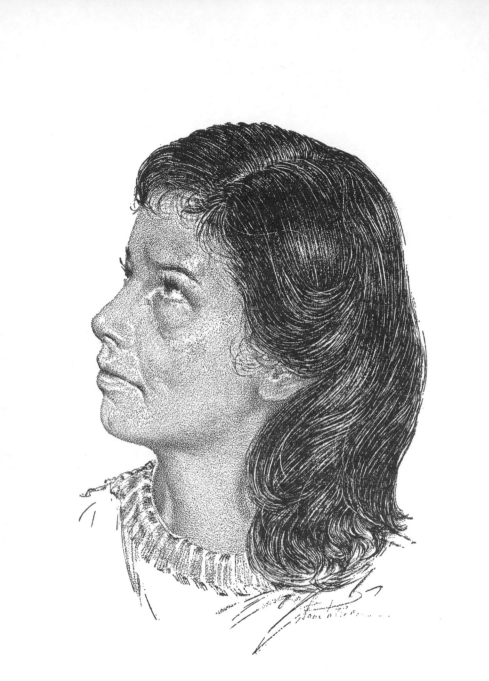

THE GIRL RESTORED

"And he took the damsel by the hand, and said unto her, Talitha cumi; which is, being interpreted, Damsel, I say unto thee, arise!"

—*Mark V:41*

L UKE TELLS US that this girl, daughter of Jairus, was about twelve years old, but he does not divulge the nature of her illness nor give her name.

Her father, the governor of a synagogue, sought Jesus out, asking Him to heal his only daughter. But even as he was asking help, a messenger arrived from his house telling him that the girl was already dead. Jesus, however, told the anxious father that he need not fear. "Believe only, and she shall be made whole."

When He came to the house with Jairus, funeral ceremonies were already in progress. But again Jesus reassured the grieving parent. "The damsel is not dead, but sleepeth."

By this, He apparently meant that her soul was not so far departed that He could not summon it again into the body, for when Jesus took her by the hand and told her to arise, Luke says:

"Her spirit came again, and she arose straightway."

Jesus then directed that she be given food to restore her depleted physical energy.

Her parents were naturally astonished because, although they had faith that Jesus might heal her of her illness, they had little hope that He could bring her back from the dead.

Jesus cautioned them "that they should tell no man what was done."

Some Bible scholars say that He enjoined secrecy because the time of His suffering and death had not yet come; and He did not want to provide a pretext for the rulers to conspire against Him.

THE CENTURION

"Now when the centurion saw what was done, he glorified God, saying, Certainly this was a righteous man."

—*Luke XXIII:47*

A CENTURION, as the name indicates, was an officer in the Roman army, who commanded a hundred soldiers.

Scripture tells us very little of the Centurion who rode at the head of the tragic procession which escorted Jesus to Calvary to be crucified.

We know that he rode a horse and that after him, among the Roman legionaries, came Jesus and the two thieves who were to be executed with Him.

Following them came the jeering mass of men, women, and even children who pressed around Him with words of cruel mockery and abuse.

It is evident from the hints given us in the Biblical account that the Centurion, like Pilate, had no enthusiasm for his task. From time to time, he turned around to look back at the Man of Sorrows.

Physically depleted by the previous night of questioning and beatings, His face blotched with blood, Jesus struggled under the weight of His Cross.

When He fell beneath its weight, the Centurion ordered two soldiers to help Him back to His feet. Then the Roman officer looked about in the crowd for someone to bear the Cross. On one face he saw pity and grief and disgust. It was the face of Simon, a man from Cyrenia.

So he commanded the stranger to bear the Cross. Simon gladly complied, and the sad procession shuffled on toward the limestone hill outside Jerusalem. Because the powdery white mound resembled a skull, it was called Golgotha.

With growing uneasiness, the Centurion carried out his orders. But as the grisly business proceeded, he noted a strange oppression within himself. Or had he imagined it? Looking upon the One who hung limp upon the crude wooden cross, blood still flowing from His wounds, the Centurion asked himself: Why is this man so different from others who have been crucified? Then a strange awareness came upon him; "Certainly, this was a righteous man."